TRIM-LIFE®
Weight Release Program

Developed by
Diane Zimberoff, M.A.

Offered exclusively through

Published by Wellness Press
TRIM-LIFE® National Headquarters
The Wellness Institute
3716 - 274th Avenue SE
Issaquah, WA 98029
Telephone (425) 391-9716 or 800-326-4418

Fifth printing 2006
Printed in the United States of America

The information in this book is not intended as medical advice. Its intention is solely informational and educational. It is recommended that the reader consult a medical or health professional should the need for one be warranted.

CONTENTS

A WORD
FROM THE AUTHOR

Hello, I'm Diane Zimberoff and I would like to introduce myself and the TRIM-LIFE PROGRAM.

I have a Masters Degree in Marriage, Family, and Child Counseling and have been in the field of human services for over thirty years. In 1984 I discovered that I could be far more effective as a therapist by adding hypnosis to my practice.

For much of my life, I struggled with weight, going up and down like a yo-yo. When I became a certified hypnotherapist, I began to see results with my own weight-loss, but it still was not consistent enough.

As I continued my research and treatment of clients with eating disorders, I realized that some of my eating habits were just as compulsive as some bulimics. I realized that if I could find "the solution" for myself, it would certainly help my clients as well.

Finally, out of desperation, I attended a training session by Dr. Donald Keppner. In my own personal work with Dr. Keppner, I discovered the "secret" to compulsive eating problems - the underlying emotions that were being "stuffed down" with food. At last my eating was under control! And that's when I developed the TRIM-LIFE PROGRAM.

I had helped myself and was excited to help others. It was so gratifying to continue with my own changes and to see the same changes in my clients. Finally I had an answer to the age-old weight control problem!

Now you too can create the same exciting personal success but with a whole lot less work because the research and methodology has been done and proven! The TRIM-LIFE PROGRAM is the most exciting event in my thirty-year professional career.

I'm delighted by the opportunity to share this dynamic new program with you. It gives **you** the opportunity to experience that "Diets don't work, hypnosis does!"

PROGRAM PHILOSOPHY

"I feel like a failure! I've been on every diet available and nothing seems to work for me. There must be something wrong with me."

It is becoming common knowledge that, for the majority of people, diets just don't work. In fact, the studies are showing that diets actually make people gain weight. It has been shown that if you take skinny people and put them on and off diets, they will actually gain weight. The key to this statement is "on and off." How many diets have you been on and off?

In his book *Diets Don't Work,* Bob Schwartz talks about a clinic he runs for those very underweight people who have trouble gaining weight. He puts them on a diet and they are appalled. "I came here to gain weight, not to lose it!" they say. The first three days, they may lose five to seven pounds; they are horrified. They are then taken off the diet and allowed to eat normally. Guess what happens. They immediately put the weight back on and then some.

Then Mr. Schwartz puts them back on another diet. This time they lose less - maybe three or four pounds. When they go off of the diet again and start eating normally, guess what happens this time. You guessed it; they put it all back on and even more excess than they did the last time. The next time they go on the diet, many don't lose anything at all, but when they start eating normally they continue to put on more and more weight.

This finding is not shocking to those of us who have been dieting most of our lives. We have experienced it ourselves millions of times. We have experienced the fact that diets work - but in reverse! That over the years, the more diets we've gone on, the more weight we seem to gain in the long run. We never understood why and we always thought it was our own fault.

This pattern has probably made you feel like a failure. Perhaps you've been thinking, "What's wrong with me? Why can't I lose weight? I probably don't have enough will power. Or maybe there is something physically wrong with me." You've probably used all the excuses and rationalizations imaginable to justify the fact that you keep dieting and losing and gaining!

In primitive times and in other countries, there were famines where little or no food was available for long periods of time. Because of that, the body has developed a way of "holding on to fat" when it thinks it is starving. This is a survival mechanism which has served us well in the past but gets in our way when we try to lose weight.

This "holding on to fat" is often referred to as the "set-point" theory. And this whole principle is one of the main reasons why diets don't work. Most diets are set up for people to lose a lot of weight quickly. When this happens, the body "thinks" it's starving and begins trying to protect itself from dying with this process.

Many of you have been taught **DIET THINKING** or **THE DIET MENTALITY** ever since you were very young. Women, especially as young girls, become very preoccupied with looking thin and attractive. The pressure to fit into certain standards of beauty begins to build at a very young age. So girls start reading magazines which are filled with diets. Or mothers, obsessed with their own weight, put their daughters on diets to try to prevent later problems.

The diet mentality puts the fear of fat into people: fat is bad and thin is good. Therefore if you are fat, you automatically feel like a failure. This fear of being fat, i.e., "bad," causes you to feel more and more pressure to lose weight. Since the only way you know how to lose weight is by dieting, then there is more and more pressure to diet. Since many people eat when they feel under pressure, this in itself can cause you to fail.

Most diets that you read or hear about promise large weight losses quickly. And so with the diet mentality we have been programmed to try to lose as much as we can as quickly as possible. Going back to the set-point theory that the body panics if too much is lost too quickly, we are again setting ourselves up for failure. In order to release weight you must drop all this diet thinking.

The **TRIM-LIFE PROGRAM** is **NOT A DIET!** This is a

weight release program designed to teach you how to release weight without dieting. This is a different way of thinking since most of you probably have thought that dieting was the only way to release weight. THAT IS NOT TRUE! We want you to get out of DIET THINKING because that will only defeat you.

Another set of reasons why diets don't work are all the psychological ones. When you go on a diet, you think of it as something *temporary*. Your mind accepts the diet as something you have to do for a limited time period and then you can go back to the way it was before - back to your old comfort zone. As we've mentioned before, when you go off of a diet and back to old eating habits, you tend to gain all the weight back plus more.

For many of us, food was used as a reward when we were children. So the diet, which in our mind feels like the absence of food, becomes like a punishment. Have you ever lost ten pounds and felt like you did so good that you deserved a reward? So you may have gone and gotten an ice cream cone or some other sweet "goodie." This is another reason why diets don't work, because they set up the cycle of punishment and reward in our minds. When you get tired of feeling like you're being punished all the time with food, that's when you can't seem to face another diet.

Another key element in THE DIET MENTALITY is the cycle of deprivation and indulgence. People who have been overweight have usually deprived themselves of fun as well as food. Because of feeling fat, you may have restricted summer activities which called for bathing suits or shorts. You may avoid social gatherings where food will be present, often times feeling self-conscious eating in front of others. When you restrict yourself, you then set up the feeling of being deprived. When you feel too deprived, the response is often to turn to food. And thus the mental cycle of dieting is deprivation and then indulging.

The vicious cycle of DIET FAILURE also plays a major role in why diets don't work. When people are asked about their experience with dieting, they usually look down at the floor as if to say they are ashamed. Perhaps this is you. You have been on so many diets and failed, that you can't stand to face another failure.

You can't look at another calorie counter or a piece of paper with two ounces of this and four ounces of that. And yet the fear of not being on a diet is worse.

This cycle of panic gets worse the more diets you go on and the more times they don't work for you. You go off the diet and begin gaining weight and the panic gets worse. The more panic you feel, the greater the tendency to binge. And as this cycle continues to worsen, you become more obsessed with weight and scales and tight-fitting clothes and cookies and junk food.

The worst part of this cycle is that you begin to take it personally. You begin to feel that you are the failure. This process begins to chisel away at your self-esteem. No matter how motivated you are or how strict you are, you seem to be defeated. So you conclude that there is something wrong with you. And this becomes yet another vicious cycle; the lower your self-esteem the more difficult success becomes. It is very difficult to succeed at anything when your self-image is so low, especially dieting!

Another reason why the diet mentality is so self-defeating is that dieters give away the control in their lives. When you go on Dr. X's diet, you are no longer in control of what, when and how much you eat.

You are giving your problem and also your control over to Dr. X. When you give him the power in your life, you are remaining a helpless victim. You also can then blame him for your inevitable failure: "Dr. X's diet just didn't work. I think I'd better try Dr. Y's diet."

When you give away your power about releasing weight, you also give away your power about what you are eating. So now you can blame it all on Baskin-Robbins or Famous Amos. You feel out of control with your body and with food. There is no way that you can solve a problem in your life when you are not taking responsibility for it in the first place. The diet mentality propagates this idea that you can't make your own choices - that you are helpless in your own life.

The last reason that diets don't work relates to another vicious cycle. This is the cycle of guilt. When we were young our parents often made us feel guilty about not eating all of the food on our plates. "You'd better eat all that food on your plate, think of all those starving children in Africa," they would chide. Or, "I've sweated all day over a hot stove to make your favorite meal, and now you sit there not eating." There is only one thing that would get rid of those horrible pangs of guilt we were feeling in our stomachs - to eat the food!

This is exactly how the vicious cycle of guilt was set up. How many times have you gone on a diet and not eaten exactly what you were supposed to eat? You then begin to feel guilty and by evening you are eating everything that isn't nailed down. This is very common in dieting because guilt is built into the process. Doctors and diet counselors are notorious for making people feel guilty about what they do or do not eat. This actually has the opposite result of what they are trying to accomplish. Because the cycle of guilt and food was taught to you very early on in life, you don't even need a diet counselor to make you feel guilty - you know how to do it to yourself!

How the TRIM-LIFE PROGRAM Is Different From Diets

The TRIM-LIFE PROGRAM is not something that you go on and off. With this program, you will learn to change your eating habits permanently. You will learn to think and feel like a thin person. You will make choices as thin people do and you will begin to act like a thin person. Through the use of hypnosis, you will be able to change your mental attitude about food and eating.

With the TRIM-LIFE PROGRAM you will never feel punished as you have on diets before. We will spend a great deal of energy teaching you how to love yourself regardless of what you weigh. It is important for you to learn that you are lovable and that you do deserve love. As your self-esteem begins to grow, you no longer have to punish yourself with destructive eating habits. You no longer have to punish yourself because you don't fit into the image of "Miss America."

In the TRIM-LIFE PROGRAM you will never feel deprived.

The reason is that we teach you to get back in touch with your body. We have a technique which will be programmed into your subconscious mind, that will help you determine exactly how hungry you are and when it is time for you to eat. Therefore you will not be depriving yourself.

You will never feel deprived because you can eat any time you feel hungry. We will teach you the difference between true hunger, that is physiological hunger, and mental/emotional hunger which is something totally different. And this is how you will be losing the weight. When you begin to see how much mental and emotional hunger you have been feeding, you will understand why diets haven't worked for you.

The TRIM-LIFE PROGRAM is the only weight release program that deals with the emotions connected to compulsive eating. Do you feel like a compulsive eater? Fill out the questionnaire at the end of this chapter to help you determine whether you are. The basis for compulsive eating always goes back to the emotions and the subconscious mind. This is why traditional diets and all the chains of dieting centers are unsuccessful for so many people.

During Week 3 of this program, we teach you how to identify the specific emotions that seem to trigger uncontrolled eating for you. We then teach you how to extinguish those old unproductive feelings. We also teach you how to express your emotions in a healthy way so that you no longer have to use food to repress those feelings.

You will learn how to use the hypnosis for motivation. Because you feel like you have failed so often on diets, you have probably concluded that you have no will power. Nothing could be further from the truth. You have had the will power and determination to try hundreds of diets even in the face of continued defeat. And in spite of all that you haven't given up. It is exactly that same will power and determination that has gotten you to this program. And it is exactly that determination which will take you to success. Again, it's not that you don't have will power, it is the diet thinking that has defeated you.

QUESTIONNAIRE ON COMPULSIVE EATING

*Questions with 2 choices (over- or under-eating),
circle the correct one for you.*

Yes No

❏ ❏ 1. Do you constantly think about food or your next opportunity to eat?

❏ ❏ 2. Have you made mistakes at work or school because you were thinking of bingeing on food?

❏ ❏ 3. Do you spend too much money on food?

❏ ❏ 4. Do you plan your day around getting food?

❏ ❏ 5. Do you have the need for a binge after a period of time when you could not eat?

❏ ❏ 6. Do you finish before everyone else or feel like you inhale your food?

❏ ❏ 7. Do you eat your food in a ritualistic manner?

❏ ❏ 8. Do you go to the store for one thing and come out with extra?

❏ ❏ 9. Have you ever eaten something that normally you would find disgusting: stale cookie, something you've put in the garbage, a still-frozen pie or pizza?

❏ ❏ 10. Do you hide food in the house, drawers, your car, your desk?

❏ ❏ 11. Have you ever made excuses for overeating?

❏ ❏ 12. Have you lied about how much or how little food you had eaten?

❏ ❏ 13. Do you get angry if someone comments on your eating or weight?

❏ ❏ 14. Have you become verbally abusive or avoidant with family or friends because of their comments about your weight or food?

❏ ❏ 15. Do you see yourself as thinner or heavier than others see you?

❏ ❏ 16. Do you feel confused when over- or under-eating?

Yes   No

❑   ❑   17. If you feel fat, do you think that you are no good?

❑   ❑   18. Have you been embarrassed by someone catching you binging/purging or throwing away food?

❑   ❑   19. Have you stopped eating (fasted) for two days or more to control eating/weight?

❑   ❑   20. Have your values been compromised?

❑   ❑   21. Have you experienced an increased tolerance for over-eating, i.e., does it take more and more to satisfy you?

❑   ❑   22. Do you experience periods when you cannot stop eating except by interruption or sleep?

❑   ❑   23. Have you tried several weight loss/food control methods or diets?

❑   ❑   24. Have others expressed concerns about your eating, weight, or behaviors around food?

❑   ❑   25. Have you experienced the shakes, tremors, feeling as though you may pass out?

❑   ❑   26. If you eat sugar or carbohydrate foods, do you crave more?

❑   ❑   27. Have you ever put food (getting or avoiding it) before a friend, spouse, child?

❑   ❑   28. Can you think back to times as a child or now when food seemed like a friend or enemy?

❑   ❑   29. Have you identified an emotional emptiness that seems to get bigger each time you over-eat?

❑   ❑   30. Do you feel shame about your eating or not eating?

❑   ❑   31. Do you go through drive-throughs so people won't see you or go to different places so you won't be recognized?

❑   ❑   32. Do you experience a "high" when you eat?

❑   ❑   33. Have you been unaware of finishing an entire container of something until after it was all gone?

❑   ❑   34. Do you collect calorie counters, recipes, cookbooks, the latest diet books?

Yes No

☐ ☐ 35. Are there times when you hate your body or a part of your body?

☐ ☐ 36. Have you wished that you would die to end the circle of eating and dieting?

☐ ☐ 37. Is it difficult or impossible for you to leave food on your plate?

☐ ☐ 38. If there is something in the house that you enjoy eating, do you think about it so much that you finally have to eat it?

☐ ☐ 39. Do you feel as if food controls you, rather than the other way around?

☐ ☐ 40. Have you ever or do you now binge and throw up? (If so, please make this known immediately.)

Do you hide what you eat from others? Describe.

_____

_____

_____

_____

Describe any other compulsive eating habits that you are aware of.

_____

_____

_____

_____

_____

DO YOU HAVE THE DIET MENTALITY?
(Write about these questions in your journal)

1. When did you first start dieting?

2. How many diets have you been on since then (approximately)?

3. How much did you weigh when you first started to diet?

4. How much do you weigh now?

5. Do you feel guilty when you eat something good?

6. Do you say, "I'll start tomorrow"?

7. Do you dream of going to bed fat and waking up thin?

8. Do you hate or dislike yourself?

9. When you eat do you think you are "cheating"?

10. Do you feel guilty when you are not on a diet?

TAKING A LOOK AT YOUR EATING HABITS

1. Do you eat while reading or watching television?

2. Are you sometimes surprised when you look down and the food is gone, having little or no awareness of eating it?

3. Do you "inhale" your food as if someone else would take it away from you if you didn't eat it quickly?

4. Do you often take second and third helpings?

5. Do you sometimes eat and realize that you haven't even tasted your food?

6. Do you often eat on the run? standing up? in your car? or somewhere other than sitting down at the table?

PARTICIPANT'S EVALUATION

Pre-Testing Date _____   Post-Testing Date _____

1. STRESS LEVEL RATING   ___ (Pre-)___ (Post-)
       0—Very high
       1—Quite a lot
       2—Moderate amount
       3—More than slight amount
       4—Slight amount
       5—No stress

2. ABILITY TO CONTROL STRESS   ___ (Pre-)___ (Post-)
       0—Totally unable
       1—Slightly able to control it
       2—Sometimes control it well
       3—Usually control it well
       4—Almost always control it well
       5—Always control it well

3. SELF-ESTEEM RATING   ___ (Pre-)___ (Post-)
       0—Do not like myself at all
       1—I like myself a very small amount
       2—Do like myself somewhat
       3—Like myself more than somewhat
       4—Almost always like myself
       5—Like everything about myself

4. PARTICIPATION WITH SUGAR   ___ (Pre-)___ (Post-)
       0—Totally out of control with sugar
       1—Usually out of control
       2—Often out of control
       3—Sometimes out of control
       4—Occasionally out of control
       5—No attraction to sugar

5. PARTICIPATION WITH CAFFEINE   ___ (Pre-)___ (Post-)
    0—10 to 30+ cups of coffee/pop/tea per day
    1—2 to 10 cups every day
    2—1 cup of coffee or pop per day
    3—3 to 4 times per week
    4—one per week
    5—no caffeine at all

6. PARTICIPATION WITH ALCOHOL   ___ (Pre-)___ (Post-)
    0—Totally out of control with alcohol
    1—Drink 4 to 5 times per week
    2—Drink only on weekends
    3—Once per week
    4—Drink occasionally
    5—Alcohol is out of my life

7. PARTICIPATION WITH NICOTINE   ___ (Pre-)___ (Post-)
    0—Over 2 packs per day addicted
    1—One pack per day
    2—1/2 pack per day
    3—Less than 1 /2 pack per day
    4—Smoke occasionally
    5—Never smoke

8. PARTICIPATION WITH VITAMINS   ___ (Pre-)___ (Post-)
    0—Never take them
    1—Take them periodically in my life
    2—Only when I am sick
    3—Try to take them but usually forget
    4—Forget only once in awhile
    5—Take on a daily basis

9. PARTICIPATION WITH EXERCISE   ___ (Pre-)___ (Post-)
    0—Never exercise
    1—Periodically exercise
    2—Exercise less than once a week
    3—30 minutes to 1 hour, 1 to 3 times per week
    4—30 minutes to 1 hour, 3 times per week
    5—30 minutes to 1 hour per day, every day

10. OVERALL HEALTH RATING ___ (Pre-)___ (Post-)
    0—Several major illnesses
    1—1 major illness
    2—Sick over 10 times per year
    3—Sick 4 to 10 times per year
    4—Sick 2 times or less per year
    5—Never get sick

11. FEMALE CONDITIONS (Women Only) ___ (Pre-)___ (Post-)
    0—Change of life (over)
    1—In the middle of change of life
    2—Total hysterectomy
    3—Partial hysterectomy
    4—Tubal ligation
    5—Birth control pills

12. CONTROL OF HORMONES ___ (Pre-)___ (Post-)
    0—Totally controlled by my hormones
    1—Experience many of these symptoms every month
        (depression, headaches, insomnia, anger)
    2—Experience symptoms often
    3—Experience symptoms sometimes
    4—Experience symptoms rarely
    5—Totally in control of my hormones

13. MEDICATIONS ___ (Pre-)___ (Post-)
    0—On 6 or more medications per day
    1—On 5 to 6 per day
    2—On 4 to 5 per day
    3—On 2 to 3 per day
    4—On one medication per day
    5—No medication at all

WEEK 1

A. LEARNING TO SET APPROPRIATE GOALS

Most of you, as we discussed in the introduction, have lost weight many times before. If you come to this program and your only goal is to lose weight, then you probably will do just that. If you would like the benefits to be more long lasting and far reaching than just losing weight, you must expand your goals. We have many goals for our participants which we would like to share with you. We hope that you will relate to these goals and choose them for your own. We put these goals in the form of affirmations since this will help you to incorporate them in your life. Choose a new one each week to write out 25 times per day.

1. I easily release the extra weight from my body.

2. I release weight by changing my eating habits permanently.

3. I easily incorporate a daily exercise program into my life.

4. Because I care about myself, I choose healthy, nutritious food.

5. I take total responsibility for my life, my body, and the food that I eat.

6. I am totally committed to learning new and healthy ways to express my emotions.

7. I easily achieve and maintain a healthy weight for the rest of my life.

8. The more I love myself, the more love I have to give to others.

9. Because I am a successful person, I easily achieve my goals.

10. I am dedicated to the process of opening up to the real me.

These affirmations will become an important part of your program. Choose one each week and use it for that entire week. Copy it on a 3 x 5 card and put it up in places where you are likely to see it. Repeat your affirmations as often as possible. Instead of filling your head with negative, worried thoughts, replace them with these positive affirmations.

B. SUCCESSFUL PEOPLE

Because you have been on so many diets and failed, you probably have difficulty thinking of yourself as a successful person. It is now time to realize that it is the whole system of dieting that is in itself the failure. You have not failed, the diet has.

It's important to begin thinking of yourself as a successful person so that you can be successful with the TRIM-LIFE PROGRAM. There are certain characteristics of successful people.

1.   They take risks.

2.   They make changes.

3.   They turn failure into a learning experience.

Just by the fact that you are here, we know that you are a successful person. You have taken the risk to do something different. You are trying something new - hypnosis. You have taken a risk. You want a change in your life because you know that in order to lose weight, you are going to have to change. You are here and that in itself tells us that you are a successful person.

C. FOOD, OUR LINK TO THE PAST

Food in our culture is used for many different purposes. It is used as a pain killer. When children are little, they hear constantly, "Here, eat this, it will make you feel better." So we begin to think of food as a way to solve problems or to avoid them.

Food is also used as a reward. Often times we say to our

children, "Now if you are a very good little girl, Mommy will buy you an ice cream." Thus we learn to think of food as a reward, and as we get older we use it to reward ourselves. We must learn to reward ourselves with something other than food.

Many of us use food as a comfort or as a way to nurture ourselves. This often stems from childhood when our parents may have used food as a substitute for their love. An example is a mother who works and feels guilty, so she bakes cookies and cakes for the child to have when she or he comes home to an empty house after school. So you become used to this pattern of "coming home and eating" and using food as a comfort.

Food also links us to our past as a symbol of family closeness. Many families do not know how to express love by open affection. They may feel uncomfortable saying the words, "I love you." So they say it with food. Food also becomes a way of reducing guilt. A mother will spend days cooking and putting her love into the food she prepares. If you don't eat it, then Mama feels rejected. Mama makes you feel guilty, as if you don't love her anymore, so you eat the food to reduce your guilt.

Many of us heard about all the starving children in India, or wherever, and spent many nights sitting at the table feeling guilty while staring at a pile of cold peas! We eventually ate the food, but felt angry, helpless and out of control.

Food then becomes an issue of control. Many parents use food as a means of showing kids who's boss! "You will sit there and not leave until you eat everything on your plate!" This stern command is meant to show us that we do not have control of our lives or our bodies. This is when we begin to sneak food or develop compulsive eating patterns in an attempt to show them or ourselves that we can control our own lives.

Food also is used as a health issue. If you're sick, it's because you're too thin or you don't eat enough. The concept that fat babies are healthy babies is nonsense and yet we have all been programmed in our delicate subconscious minds to believe this.

In order to release weight, we must separate food from all of these issues and begin to see it objectively for what it really is: fuel for the body. We must realize that food is not our mother; that food does not love us or take away loneliness. We must realize that food is not our friend or our reward for being good. Food is just the substance that keeps us going.

D. HYPNOSIS: THE MAJOR TOOL FOR WEIGHT RELEASE

1. Dispelling the myths of hypnosis

Can anyone be hypnotized?

Yes, anyone and everyone can be hypnotized, as long as they want to be. You cannot be hypnotized against your will. Hypnosis is a shifting from the conscious to the subconscious part of the mind. Hypnosis is a natural state of mind, and all people spend from 50 percent to 80 percent of their time in the subconscious mind. An example of this is staring at the road while driving a long distance. You may become aware that you really haven't seen anything for a long period of time; you may think, "Where have I been?" You have been in a light state of hypnosis, in your subconscious mind.

Another example of being in hypnosis while you think you are awake may be if you are staring at the television or the computer for a time. Have you ever stood there talking to your children or husband while they were watching television and they didn't seem to hear a word you said? They weren't ignoring you; they were in a light state of hypnosis.

Just as the old-time hypnotists would have someone stare at the moving watch chain to hypnotize them, it is "eye fixation" that puts you into hypnosis. And you don't have to have your eyes closed to be in that state of mind. When you try to talk to your kid and he seems kind of "spaced out"—guess where he's at? In his subconscious mind; kids go there a lot.

Will someone else be in control of my mind?

No! Once you understand hypnosis and the power of suggestion, you are the one who will be in control of your mind.

Hypnosis gives you back control of your subconscious mind. Knowledge is power and the more knowledge you have about how your mind works, the more power you have in your life. Once you understand the principles of hypnosis, you will never again allow someone else to control your mind.

What if I can't come out of it?

There is no such thing as not coming out of it. The subconscious mind will automatically switch back into the conscious mind. So if you were hypnotized and the hypnotist left the room without returning, after awhile you would come back to consciousness on your own. There has never been a case of someone "not coming back." Remember, hypnosis is a natural state of mind.

Are you going to make me cluck like a chicken? I don't want to make a fool of myself.

In hypnosis you would never do anything that was against your morals or beliefs. You must remember that there is a big difference between stage hypnosis and therapeutic hypnosis. Stage hypnosis is done for entertainment. Therapeutic hypnosis is done to change behavior. In stage hypnosis the people who volunteer are doing so because they want to get laughs. Perhaps they have never had the guts to get up on the stage but have always wanted to do so; hypnosis gives them the courage to do it. They still would never do anything against their morals. So if the hypnotist asked them to take off their clothes, they would not do it.

Therapeutic hypnosis is the most fantastic tool for changing behavior that is known to us today. It is used for weight loss, to stop smoking and to improve many other areas of our lives. Now that you are going to learn hypnosis, you are putting yourself in the forefront of personal growth and advancement.

If I open my mind with hypnosis, will the devil get in?

Totally untrue! There are many people who, because of their fears of the devil, are actually empowering the devil. In other words, the more power you give to the devil (or negative thoughts), the more power that negative thought has in your life. If you believe in God, and empower God in your life, then that is what you will have in your life. For anyone who believes in God, hypnosis actually helps to make that connection stronger.

2. The conscious versus the subconscious mind

Even though we seem to use our conscious mind a great deal of the time, there is another part of our mind that is functioning on a much larger scale. This is called the subconscious mind. It is in operation all the time, even though we are not aware of it. For example, one of the functions of the subconscious mind is to control all of the involuntary bodily functions. You never have to remind yourself to breathe or to make sure your heart beats; the subconscious takes care of all that for you.

In effect, the conscious mind is about 10 percent of the mind, due to its limited functioning. Basically, the conscious mind thinks and analyzes and has a short-term memory bank. The subconscious mind, however, has at least five functions.

The subconscious mind is just like a computer. It has a long-term memory bank where it stores an unbelievable amount of material. Contained in the subconscious mind is every event, every emotion, every sensory experience that has ever occurred in one's lifetime. And with the proper instruction, the subconscious mind can be trained for almost instant recall.

Another function of this incredible computer is to store all the emotions. It is the emotional center of the brain. So it is here in the subconscious mind that the emotions can be experienced, changed and accepted. You may wonder how emotions can be changed; we will learn that in Week 3.

The subconscious mind also holds all the habits. This is why hypnosis works to change habits. Most people try to change their habits on the conscious level of functioning and that is the reason why they are so unsuccessful. The habits are not stored or located in the conscious part of the mind. You must learn how to get into the subconscious part of the mind in order to change habits.

All the involuntary bodily functions are located in the subconscious part of the mind. So through hypnosis, we can teach you to lower your blood pressure, even out your blood-sugar level, and balance out your hormones. People are also able to get rid of headaches and eliminate insomnia. Creativity is also located in the subconscious part of the mind. This part of your mind uses images, sensations and feelings to create. It can be used for goal setting since once an image is established, the subconscious mind will take that image as a command and go forward with it. This is one reason why you will be taught to control the negative images in your mind, because the subconscious will also interpret these as commands.

3. The signs of hypnosis

The first sign of hypnosis is that your breathing will be very relaxed. You will breathe just as you do when you are asleep, called the "hypnotic sigh."

The next sign is the "hypnotic cast," the look of deep relaxation on the face of the person. During our demonstration you will see this look become even more pronounced as deepening takes place.

The body temperature in most people changes when they enter a state of hypnosis. You can feel the palm of their hands and discover that they are either very warm or very cool.

During our demonstration, you will begin to understand the power of suggestion. The subconscious mind will accept and act on suggestions that are to your benefit or that won't harm you in any way. Because it does not think or analyze, it just responds to commands. It will not, however, respond to any commands that are against your better interest or morals. The power of suggestion is one of the main components of the subconscious mind which makes this program work. It will get you off junk foods and get you to your goal. Once you understand it, the uses are limitless.

Rapid eye movement is a hypnotic reaction which some people experience and others don't. When you awake, you may also experience eye lacmentation. This is a redness or blurry look in the eyes.

Some people experience feeling very light just like they are floating; others feel very heavy and swear they cannot move.

Each person's experience is different, so we do not want you to compare yourself to someone else. Just become aware of how hypnosis feels to you. There is no right or wrong and you will not be graded. If you keep thinking, "I can't do it" or "This isn't working for me," that is just your conscious mind giving you your own usual self-doubts. Returning to the words "calm and relaxed" will shut off the conscious thoughts and negative self-talk.

You do not have to experience all of these signs to know that you are in hypnosis; any one of them is enough. Just the relaxation is all you need.

E. REGULATING YOUR BLOOD SUGAR LEVEL

The very first night of class, we will help you to get off sugar, caffeine, and alcohol. You will no longer have the desire for these foods or beverages. You will not have to try; there is no effort involved. Through the power of suggestion you will be repelled by these substances. This also includes junk food of any kind.

The reason this is so important in releasing weight has to do with your blood sugar level and food cravings. When you wake up in the morning and drink caffeine and/or eat something sweet, it causes your blood sugar level to take a sharp rise upwards. To regulate this, the pancreas produces enough insulin to bring it back down to normal. The problem is that often times it actually drops to below normal. You then begin feeling tired, irritated, and craving more sugar and caffeine.

Any refined carbohydrates such as all the white-flour products immediately turn to sugar in your body. Alcohol does the same. You will be choosing nutritious foods such as whole wheat products rather than the empty calories found in junk foods, candy, and alcohol.

WEEK 1 AWARENESS EXERCISES

1. List the fears or myths you had about hypnosis before the class.

    1. _____

    2. _____

    3. _____

2. List the signs of hypnosis that you experienced.

    1. _____

    2. _____

    3. _____

3. List the emotional food links that you are aware of from your past (such as eating when lonely, sad, scared, or angry).

    1. _____

    2. _____

    3. _____

4. What messages about food have you given your children or grandchildren that you will now change?

    1. _____

    2. _____

    3. _____

    4. _____

WEEKLY INSTRUCTIONS

1. Listen to your Week 1 tape or CD at least once per day. You can do it more often if you like, but at least once per day will bring you the best results.
2. Establish a comfortable place where you will not be disturbed. Let other family members know that when you are doing your tapes, **YOU ARE NOT TO BE DISTURBED!** This is very important.
3. Play your tapes or CDs at the same time each day, if possible. This is the way to establish a habit.
4. Give yourself the suggestion that you will stay conscious, if you find that you are sleeping through the tape. If you hear the wake up, then you are not asleep, you are just in a deep state of hypnosis.
5. You can take your tapes to work and do them on a break time or at lunch. This will give you an extra spurt of energy during the day.
6. Write out what you eat each day. Keep a small simple notebook, and just jot down everything including drinks. This will keep you conscious.
7. Write out any affirmations you choose **25 times each day**.

- I am becoming more calm and relaxed now.
- All desire for sweet, white-starchy, greasy or salty foods is GONE.
- I only eat when my body is hungry - I stop when my body is satisfied.
- I am satisfied with small well-balanced meals and I always leave food on my plate.
- Therefore I enjoy feeling my stomach shrinking to its normal size, the size of my fist.
- I am healthier, happier, and trimmer each and every day of my life!

RECORD OF RELAXATION

Rate yourself on this 10-point scale before and after you do your relaxation exercise.

1. totally relaxed, no tension
2. very relaxed
3. moderately relaxed
4. fairly relaxed
5. slightly relaxed
6. slightly tense
7. fairly tense
8. moderately tense
9. very tense
10. extremely tense (the most uncomfortable you could be)

Week of	before session	after session	comments
Monday			
Tuesday			
Wednesday			
Thursday			
Friday			
Saturday			
Sunday			

Week of	before session	after session	comments
Monday			
Tuesday			
Wednesday			
Thursday			
Friday			
Saturday			
Sunday			

Week of	before session	after session	comments
Monday			
Tuesday			
Wednesday			
Thursday			
Friday			
Saturday			
Sunday			

Week of	before session	after session	comments
Monday			
Tuesday			
Wednesday			
Thursday			
Friday			
Saturday			
Sunday			

WEEK 2

I. CHANGING YOUR METABOLIC RATE

A. DEFINITION OF "METABOLISM"

Your metabolism refers to all of the biochemical processes through which the food you eat is broken down. When the food is broken down, it is then transformed into the energy you need for your daily activity. Some people have a "thrifty" metabolism while others have a "wasteful" metabolism. This wastefulness can actually be measured in the laboratory, because "wasteful" cells give off more heat than do "thrifty" cells. People who have been thin all their lives have "wasteful" cells and people who have been fat have "thrifty" cells.

If you have thrifty cells, it means that after the energy from the food is made available for bodily processes, there is an extra amount left over to be put into the fat cells for storage. Having this "thrifty trait" was great when we were faced with famine in earlier times, but it doesn't work to your advantage for weight loss.

Can you change your metabolism and the way that you burn up the food you eat? The answer is yes. Through this program, you will learn how to change your metabolism so that it will be working for you instead of against you. By changing the types of food you eat and adding exercise to your daily routine, you can change your body from a fat storehouse to a **fat-burning machine**.

B. CREEPING OBESITY

We Americans have been sold a bill of goods concerning all the "labor saving devices" that we supposedly need. For years now companies have been "spoiling" the American worker with gadgets to make life easier. The problem is that in doing that, we have become more and more sedentary in our lifestyles.

Our mothers and grandmothers kneaded their own bread,

washed clothes by hand or with a wringer, and beat their carpets to clean them. They would walk or ride horses when they had to go somewhere. They were constantly burning up calories and were not as overweight as we have become.

Recent studies show that by adding labor-saving devices to your life, you will actually gain weight. By adding an extension telephone, you can gain eight pounds in a year. Secretaries who switched from a manual typewriter to a computer gained six pounds in a year! Physical activity has a cumulative effect. In other words, it is not what you do in one day or even one week that matters; it is what you do in a year and for the rest of your life. To change your metabolism and keep it changed, it is important to become an "active person" rather than a sedentary person. You can't just do some exercise until you lose weight, and then stop and expect to keep it off. Your body is like any machine; it will deteriorate rapidly when not used.

Some people who are still thinking on the short-term level, think that you have to walk pretty far to take off a pound. If you walk for 45 minutes a day, in 14 days you will lose a pound. However, if you begin to think bigger, you will realize that if you continue to walk 45 minutes a day, you will lose 26 pounds in a year!

It is important to become an active person and to start to think like an active person. Think of ways that you can waste energy rather than conserve it: walking instead of driving, taking the stairs instead of the elevator. Try to park as far away as you can instead of as close as you can. Whatever you are doing, move as much as you can.

C. THE BENEFITS OF EXERCISE

The way to develop motivation for exercise is through hypnosis. Your subconscious mind will begin to focus on the reasons that exercise is so important; this will get you past your resistance.

If I could give you a pill that did all of the following, would you take it everyday?

1. Reduce your stress
2. Even out your blood sugar level
3. Relieve depression
4. Relieve mood swings
5. Balance hormones
6. Reduce PMS symptoms
7. Speed up metabolism so you can lose weight easily
8. Reduce your appetite
9. Prevent bone deterioration (osteoporosis)
10. Prevent heart attacks and strokes
11. Regulate insulin level and prevent diabetes
12. Produce serotonin which gives you the feeling of well-being (and reduces the need for anti-depressants)

If you could take a pill to get all these benefits, would you take it every day? Of course you would! Luckily we don't have to take a pill to enjoy all of these benefits; these are the benefits of daily exercise. In fact, the more exercise you do, the fewer pills you have to take!

D. SETTING UP YOUR DAILY PHYSICAL ACTIVITY PROGRAM

1. Do what you enjoy
   a. If you are an outdoors person, you may choose walking, hiking, biking, swimming, gardening, jump-rope, tennis, skiing, etc.

   b. If you are an indoors person you may choose a rebounder, a rowing machine, exercise bicycle, audio or video exercise tapes, TV, aerobics, etc.

2. Follow your personality
   a. If you are a social person, you may enjoy team sports like

volleyball, basketball, tennis, or bowling. Or you may enjoy dancing, an aerobics class, or walking with a friend.

b. If you enjoy being with yourself, you may enjoy walking alone, a rebounder, bicycling, a video tape, or any other individual activity.

3. Forming good habits is as easy as forming bad ones. It takes 21 days to form a good habit. Try to do your physical routine at the same time every day. This helps to establish a habit.

4. You are more likely to continue your new habit if you make it enjoyable. There are several ways to guarantee enjoyment. Make certain that your mind is filled with positive thoughts rather than negative ones while you are doing your exercise. Repeat your positive response weight control suggestions as you work out. Use your affirmations over and over in your mind. Visualize yourself at your goal weight and keep that picture in your mind. This is how you reprogram your subconscious mind.

5. Add variety to keep the exercise interesting. If you are walking, take different routes on different days. You may want to use an I-Pod and add music to your workout. Or listen to your hypnosis CDs while you are walking or riding an indoor bicycle. You may want to do different activities on different days. Perhaps you will use the rebounder on Monday, Wednesday, and Friday and jog on Tuesday, Thursday, and Saturday.

6. Recognize resistance and move right through it. Sometimes we resist making changes in our life. Some part of us often wants to return to the comfort zone of old habits. The resistance may appear in the form of excuses. The most common excuse is, "I don't have enough time." When you take a look at the benefits of daily exercise, you must realize how important it is for you to make the time. You must mentally make a commitment to yourself that you want to receive all these benefits into your life.

7. To overcome resistance, it is important that you don't allow anything to get in the way of your workout time. Recognize that this is your "gift" to yourself. In your daily appointment book, write down what your exercise will be each day in the appropriate time slot. **DO NOT ALLOW ANYTHING TO GET IN THE WAY OF YOUR DAILY GIFT TO YOURSELF!** When you are on vacations or traveling, make sure that you arrange to have your time. If people are visiting your home, make certain that they are informed that you will be unavailable for an hour each day.

If for any reason you get out of your habit, immediately start again. The longer that you use excuses, the stronger the resistance will become. The sooner you start back, the easier it will be to eliminate the resistance.

II. PMS - HORMONAL IMBALANCE

A. SYMPTOMS OF HORMONAL IMBALANCE

It is very important to learn to recognize the symptoms of hormonal imbalance so that you can reduce or eliminate these symptoms. Most women have at least some symptoms of hormonal imbalance. The symptoms include:

1. Inappropriate anger or rage
2. Irritability
3. Feeling and/or acting "bitchy"
4. Anxiety, nervousness or tension - more than usual
5. Depression - crying easily over things that aren't that sad normally
6. A general feeling of unhappiness and dissatisfaction
7. Low energy
8. Headaches
9. Insomnia - can't get to sleep, or wake up in the middle of the night
10. Food cravings - craving sweet things or salty things

(hypoglycemic reactions)
11. Breast tenderness
12. Water retention—bloat
13. Acne—skin breakouts
14. Hot flashes
15. Irregular cycles

It is very important for you to chart your cycles in terms of your symptoms regularly. Make copies of the calendar found at the end of this chapter and keep them with you. Each time you become aware of a symptom, be sure to chart it. Keep this record every day for at least six months. With this program, you will be able to see these symptoms reduced or eliminated.

B. CAUSE OF HORMONAL IMBALANCE

1. Going through puberty
2. Going on and off the birth control pill
3. Having a baby
4. Breast-feeding
5. Tubal ligation
6. Hysterectomy
7. Going through the change of life

C. THE METHODS YOU WILL USE TO CONTROL YOUR HORMONES

1. Elimination of "drugs" in your life. Caffeine, sugar, tobacco, and alcohol all make the hormonal imbalance worse. Because these substances affect the blood sugar level, the symptoms of hypoglycemia (cravings) will be exaggerated with these substances. These "drugs" also destroy Vitamins B and C, which you need to handle stress. So participation in these drugs will cause more stress and depression, forcing the hormones even further out of balance. It's a vicious cycle.

2. Daily exercise is one of the best ways to keep your

hormones in balance. Review the list of benefits of exercise and you will see how these two go together. When you exercise, your body will produce serotonin, the body's natural tranquilizer. It also will alleviate the symptoms of stress, anger, depression, low energy, and low self-esteem.

3. Good nutrition helps to give your body all the nutrients it needs so that it can function properly. This will keep your hormones in better balance.

4. Vitamin supplements are essential for controlling your symptoms. A good multiple vitamin is essential, and make certain that it is yeast-free. In the vitamin part of this lesson, I will include the label of a good high-potency vitamin. B-complex is very important and should be taken three times per day if you have strong symptoms, about 200 to 300 mgs per day. Vitamin E is also essential. Start out with 400 IUs and then slowly increase to 800 IUs. This is also excellent for controlling hot flashes and can even be taken in higher doses. Consult with a local naturopath for this.

5. Hypnosis can work in two different ways to help you control your symptoms. The first way is by reducing stress. Just doing 20 minutes of hypnosis per day - listening to your tape or CD - will reduce stress. Uncontrolled stress makes PMS worse. By using your CDs, you are receiving a cumulative benefit of daily relaxation and stress reduction.

Next, as you learned in Week 1, in the subconscious part of the mind are located all of the involuntary functions of the body. This of course includes the hormones. Through the hypnosis you will learn "hormone balancing." You can actually use the power of the subconscious mind to balance out your hormones and greatly reduce or eliminate altogether any PMS symptoms.

III. VITAMIN SUPPLEMENTS
(dosages from *Prescription for Nutritional Healing*)

1. A good high-potency mega-vitamin without yeast.

2. A B-complex can be taken 2 to 3 times per day, but not after 4 pm. The B-vitamins are to reduce stress and should be balanced. If you take high doses of one B-vitamin it can throw the others out of balance. You can take extra during times of high stress, illness, or PMS symptoms. You can take 200-300 mgs. if needed per day. Doses over 2,000 mg. daily may produce toxic effects. If you are ill and want to take higher doses of vitamin B for healing, please consult a naturopath.

3. Vitamin E is important for hormonal balance for men and women. If you are on the pill, taking hormones, or going through menopause, this vitamin is essential. It is important as an anti-oxidant and research indicates that it may prevent cancer. Begin with 400 IUs and after a month increase to 800 IUs.

4. Vitamin C is very important since it helps the immune system to fight off diseases. It reduces colds and flus as well as, possibly, cancer. If you work around or live with a smoker, Vitamin C is a must – up to 3000 mg. per day. Note how much C is in your multiple vitamin and supplement the rest. Take powdered vitamin C and increase the dose by 50 mg. each day up to the point of gas or loose stools. Then cut back by 50 mg. This is the therapeutic dose for you.

5. Calcium must be balanced with Magnesium and Zinc. Take 1500 mgs. of calcium at night. The magnesium must be present *with* the calcium in order for your body to process and assimilate it. The magnesium should be half the amount of the calcium. Taken at night, this will help you sleep better and alleviate muscle cramping. Calcium is a natural relaxant.

6. Selenium is important because it works with Vitamin E to make it stronger. Check your multiple vitamin and then supplement for a dose of 200 mcg. Together with Vitamin E it reduces hardening of the arteries and some types of cancers. It is important for men as well as women.

Please consult your naturopath for your own personal vitamin/ mineral requirements.

IV. NUTRITION

A. WHAT TYPES OF FOOD DO I CHOOSE?

1. Refined carbohydrates

After Week 1, you will no longer desire refined carbohydrates such as sugar, white breads, and white pasta. You will not feel deprived of these foods, but rather you just won't be interested in them. The hypnosis will help you with that. You will find yourself making more healthy choices such as whole wheat breads, whole grain cereal, and bran products.

The nutritional goal is simply this: to eliminate the refined carbohydrates and fats in your meals. You will be replacing them with complex carbohydrates such as fresh fruits and vegetables, whole wheat and grain products, and low-fat protein. You will find yourself wanting the healthier foods and avoiding the empty calories of junk food.

2. Fats

It is important to eat a balanced amount of healthy fats. The most common fatty foods are peanut butter, cheese, butter, mayonnaise, packaged sandwich meats, and heavy salad dressings. You can use mustard instead of mayonnaise on sandwiches such as chicken and turkey. If you feel you must have cheese, grate a little on top instead of using big chunks or slices. If you must have peanut butter, spread a natural brand (with no sugar or lard added) very thinly. Olive oil is good for you, and with lemon or balsamic vinegar makes a great salad dressing. Most organic dressings such as Annie's are preferable to other heavier kinds. Check labels for low sugar. Most "low fat" foods add sugar to improve the taste. Extra sugar can cause sugar cravings.

3. Salt

It is important to lower your salt intake since sodium causes water retention as well as high blood pressure. The highest levels of sodium are found in the following:

    a. All canned and packaged foods

b. Frozen foods, especially frozen dinners
c. Most cheeses (Parmesan is okay)
d. Soda pop
e. Table salt

B. SHOPPING

Choosing the right foods begins with shopping. When you grocery shop, stay basically around the outskirts of the store. Most food stores are laid out in a similar fashion. On the outskirts you will find nonfat dairy products, fresh protein such as chicken, fish and turkey. You will also find the breads and the fresh fruits and vegetables.

Most of the foods in the aisles have been highly processed which means you are paying to have the vitamins taken out and salt, sugar, and preservatives put in. You also pay for the packaging and canning processes. The only food you may need to shop for in the aisles are cereals and whole-grain products. You may also choose brown rice, beans, and lentils as very good nonfat sources of complex carbohydrates and protein. Remember low-fat salad dressings, herbs to replace salt for seasoning, rice cakes, and wasa fiber crackers. Check in the "health food" section of your grocery store for whole wheat pasta. Don't forget the soap and recycled paper products!

C. FOOD PREPARATION

Food preparation is also very important. Stay away from fried foods or things sauteed in butter. There is no need for breading or sauces and gravies. You will begin to enjoy the natural taste of food that has been prepared in a simple and healthy way. Baking, broiling, steaming and barbecuing are best. And microwaving is excellent! Eliminate fats, sugar, and salts from your cooking. Use olive oil, lemon and herbs for flavor. Salsa is a great low fat, low sugar addition to foods.

V. THE HUNGER LEVEL

This is a very important tool in learning to determine when to eat. It is the way thin people eat all the time. With hypnosis, you will program into your mind this tool which will always be there for your use. To determine when it is time to eat, you check in with your hunger level. Begin to visualize your hunger on a continuum from 0 to 10.

0	1	**(2)**	3	4	**(5)**	6	7	8	9	10

If your hunger level is at zero, that means you have let yourself get too hungry. The zero means that you are starving, the five means just satisfied, and the ten means you are stuffed. The idea is to eat when your hunger level gets to a two (definitely hungry but not starving) and to never eat above a five. Whenever you eat above a five, you are feeding the emotions rather than the body. In this way you will be eating smaller portions and still feeling satisfied. If you let yourself get down to a zero, there is more of a tendency to want to overeat - that is, to eat above a five.

You will also be learning to shrink your stomach down to the normal size which is the size of your hand. We call this our "mental stomach bypass." This technique combined with the hunger level helps to keep your portions controlled, so you don't feel deprived as you did when you used to diet. You no longer eat by the clock or because of social pressures. You are learning to pay attention to your body and its signals.

Pay attention to your "hunger-level." Especially in the morning, you will probably be hungry enough to eat about an hour after waking. *Not eating* and thinking that you will lose weight by skipping meals is actually "stinkin' thinkin'" as they say in Alcoholics Anonymous. Skipping meals by ignoring your hunger level will only cause you to get ravenous later and will throw you into a binge.

1. The Binge-Restrict Trap

Remember the main pattern we are changing in TRIM-LIFE is the "Binge and Restrict Trap." It is a trap because every binge causes you to feel guilty, scared and desperate ... and that leads to restricting. Every restriction leads to feeling deprived and throws you into another binge. And so the trap of the binge-restrict vicious cycle continues.

If your hunger level gets down to three, have a snack. A healthy snack consists of protein and a carbohydrate. So some fresh deli meat such as turkey or chicken and a piece of fruit will bring your hunger level back to a five. A handful of nuts and a piece of fruit, natural peanut butter and half a banana, or hummus or peanut butter on a piece of celery will all bring your hunger level back to normal. These are all good snacks because they contain protein, which helps to eliminate the sugar cravings.

2. The Truth about Low Fat Foods

Most low fat foods have **LOTS** of added sugar to improve the taste. It is actually preferable NOT to use low fat foods for that reason. If you compare the labels, they may have a little less fat but notice the huge increase in sugars. *Eating* fat is not what causes you to *get* fat. It is actually sugars, which produce more insulin, which cause you to retain fat. If you want to learn more about this, read *The Zone* or *Mastering The Zone* by Barry Sears. I am not telling you to do any diet, but he does explain very well in his book about combining proteins with carbs to reduce sugar and hunger cravings. The best carbs to eat are fruits and vegetables, since they don't produce sugar cravings like junk food or empty calorie foods do.

WEEK 2 AWARENESS EXERCISES

Physical exercise program

1. Describe how much exercise you were doing before this program.

_____

_____

2. What is your <u>motivation</u> for setting up your physical routine program?

a. _____

b. _____

c. _____

d. _____

e. _____

3. State exactly what your beginning exercise program will be.

What time of the day? _____

How long? _____

What will you do? _____

What goal are you working towards in terms of amount of time, etc? _____

4. List the "excuses" you have used in the past.

a._____

b. _____

c. _____

PMS - Hormonal Imbalance

1. List the symptoms you experience on a regular basis.

a. _____

b. _____

c. _____

d. _____

e. _____

Hunger level

Check off your reasons for eating:
 a. It is a certain time (breakfast time, noon, or dinnertime).
 b. The food is there.
 c. I "might" get hungry later.
 d. Feeling lonely or bored.
 e. Procrastination - to put off doing something.
 f. Stuffing down feelings.
 g. "Grazing" - feeling dissatisfied and searching for something.
 h. Because no one else is there to see what you eat.
 i. For comfort and nurturing.
 j. As a reward for being "good."
 k. Feeling disgusted with yourself – "so what?"
 l. Someone else is paying for it, so you might as well.
 m. TV eating - watching and unconsciously stuffing yourself.
 n. Fear that there won't be any later on - scarcity or lack.
 o. Rebellion - I'm grown up and I'll eat whatever I like.
 p. Dividing up the day - coffee break gets you to lunch, which gets you to afternoon break, which gets you to dinner, which gets you to bedtime snack, etc.
 q. Pre- and post-dieting eating - stuffing yourself before and after diets.
 r. Binge eating – on occasion eating everything you can find.
 s. Stress eating - using food to try to calm yourself down.
 s. Energy eating - feeling low energy and using food to boost it.
 t. Creative eating - you use food preparation as your main creative outlet and then you feel you must eat it.
 u. Depression eating - to try to make yourself feel better.
 v. The Great Depression eating – you can't "waste" anything.

After you have checked off the ones that apply to you, use the next page to write out your specific awarenesses about why and when you have eaten in the past.

Past

1. _____

2. _____

3. _____

4. _____

5. _____

6. _____

7. _____

8. _____

More recently

1. _____

2. _____

3. _____

4. _____

5. _____

6. _____

7. _____

8. _____

CHART YOUR PMS SYMPTOMS

JANUARY						
Sun	Mon	Tue	Wed	Thu	Fri	Sat

JULY						
Sun	Mon	Tue	Wed	Thu	Fri	Sat

FEBRUARY						
Sun	Mon	Tue	Wed	Thu	Fri	Sat

AUGUST						
Sun	Mon	Tue	Wed	Thu	Fri	Sat

MARCH						
Sun	Mon	Tue	Wed	Thu	Fri	Sat

SEPTEMBER						
Sun	Mon	Tue	Wed	Thu	Fri	Sat

APRIL						
Sun	Mon	Tue	Wed	Thu	Fri	Sat

OCTOBER						
Sun	Mon	Tue	Wed	Thu	Fri	Sat

MAY						
Sun	Mon	Tue	Wed	Thu	Fri	Sat

NOVEMBER						
Sun	Mon	Tue	Wed	Thu	Fri	Sat

JUNE						
Sun	Mon	Tue	Wed	Thu	Fri	Sat

DECEMBER						
Sun	Mon	Tue	Wed	Thu	Fri	Sat

PMS HORMONAL IMBALANCE SYMPTOMS

1=1st day of cycle	BT= Breast	E = Emotional	MS = Mood swings
A = Anxiety	tenderness	F = Fatigue	0 = Ovulation
AC= Acne	C = Food cravings	H =Headaches	R = Rage, anger
B = Bloating	D = Depression	I = Insomnia	S =Shaky

WEEK 3

I. ELIMINATING "DIET THINKING"

It is very important to continue to get rid of "diet thinking." Do not go back to an old "comfortable diet" or to fasting just to lose a few extra pounds. You will be defeating yourself because the psyche will begin to feel deprived and will throw you right back into rebellion. You are not on a diet nor will you ever be on one again! You are changing your eating habits for the rest of your life.

A comfortable weight release is 1 to 3 pounds per week. This comes out to about 4 to 12 pounds per month. Your body can easily handle these changes and can adapt. Some people release more at the beginning or at different times. Some people release less. Do not get caught up in pressuring yourself about how much you have released - that is diet thinking. The important factor is that you are in control of what you eat. If you are not in control, then you must address that issue. And this week we will be doing just that.

Learn to give yourself non-food rewards. You can put the money in a jar that you would have used on junk food or more diet programs and then buy yourself some new clothes. Or put one dollar in for each pound you lose. Perhaps you have a closet full of clothes - getting to wear them is a new reward now that they are beginning to fit you. Use exercise or sports activities as rewards.

Once you stop the pressure that comes from "being on a diet" you can relax and just watch the weight come off.

II. EMOTIONAL FACTORS AND UNDERLYING CAUSES OF OVEREATING

A. "STUFFING YOUR EMOTIONS"

Another reason why diets don't work is because they never address the issue of emotions. If you ask a thin person why they eat, they will think you are crazy - they eat because they are hungry. If you ask a compulsive eater why they eat, there are usually many reasons, most of which have nothing to do with hunger.

As children in our society, we are not taught healthy ways to release emotions. We are usually taught destructive ways such as yelling and screaming (which doesn't release them - just hurts the other person); or we are taught to repress them. We get a lot of "don't feel" messages as we grow up.

1. "Don't feel" messages

The "don't feel" messages often have to do with which sex you are. Boys are not allowed to feel sad or scared. How many times have you said to your children, "Come on now, be a big boy and don't cry." Or "Big boys don't cry." What are we teaching little boys when we do this? We are teaching them to "stuff" their emotions.

This is the same thing we do to little girls, except it's okay for little girls to cry. But it's not okay for them to get angry. It's not "ladylike." Little girls are supposed to be "sugar and spice and everything nice." They are supposed to be "seen and not heard." All of these ridiculous phrases give children the message not to be real. We are taught to be phony, to repress our true feelings and to act.

B. COMPULSIVE HABITS

We learn how to "stuff our feelings" by watching the grown-ups around us. Many people with weight problems had an alcoholic parent. Using alcohol, drugs, tobacco or food to stuff down feelings is one and the same. This is the basis for compulsive habits. Every time one of the "don't feel" emotions comes to you, you run to the food, alcohol, drugs or cigarettes!

The more emotions you have to repress, the more food and drugs it takes to do so. The old image of the "happy fat person" is just a cover-up. Many times in childhood, you may have experienced traumas that were very difficult for you as a child to deal with. We're going to address the four main types of abuse that you may have experienced.

C. UNRESOLVED PAIN

As a small child, you were a very sensitive creature. Children are very perceptive and intuitive. You could feel the pain and fear of the adults around you. But as a small child, you probably didn't know what to do with all those feelings. You may have learned to turn to food to make yourself "feel better."

1. Emotional abuse

Some parents or teachers take their fear, anger, and pain out on their children. The child may represent all the things that the adult doesn't like in himself or herself. This may come out in emotional abuse. The adult may use criticisms, put downs, and name-calling to "discipline" the child, but it is actually shaming the child. The emotions which the child feels in this situation are certainly not allowed to be expressed, so they just keep getting pushed further and further down.

Emotional abuse, as all abuse, greatly affects the self-esteem of the child. If you were emotionally abused as a child, you may find yourself doing a lot of self-destructive things because underneath you may really hate yourself. If our parents and teachers didn't like us, it may be difficult for us to like ourselves. This week, you will get in touch with this and learn how to love yourself.

2. Physical abuse

Physical abuse usually involves the adult releasing his or her anger on the child. It can be with the use of a strap or belt, a switch, the fist, a boot (as in kicking), etc. It is usually done in the name of discipline. Physical abuse causes the child to fear and hate authority. The child has many feelings which must be repressed or turned inwards on him or herself. General feelings of anxiety can usually be traced back to physical abuse.

3. Neglect

Neglect happens in many different families for different reasons. It can happen in a family where both parents want to give the child more than they had when they were children. Maybe both parents are upwardly mobile and put their careers before the needs of their children. Or maybe they remember the Depression and just want their kids to have more.

Many people begin to eat as soon as they walk into their homes - hungry or not! This usually goes back to parents who substituted food for love.

You may look back on your childhood and consciously think it was pretty good and pretty normal. And that may be true; however, there may have still been a feeling of emptiness or dissatisfaction which you have been using food to fill up. This emptiness may have been some form of neglect.

4. Sexual abuse

Another form of child abuse that may have touched your life is sexual abuse. About one out of three women and one out of five men has been sexually abused as a child. Now you may wonder what that has to do with being overweight. It has everything to do with it! Many times "the child part" will make decisions out of the subconscious mind that affect you for the rest of your life. Unless these decisions are examined and changed they can continue to affect you without your knowledge.

An example of an early decision out of the subconscious mind is, "If I'm fat, no one will want me (sexually), so this won't happen again." Often children gain weight after they have been sexually abused in an attempt to prevent it from recurring. They may gain weight because they are "stuffing" their feelings about the abuse. Gaining weight is a very typical reaction to any traumatic event.

5. Grief

Another traumatic event may be the loss of someone close. In our society we are often encouraged to "stuff" our emotions. Comments such as, "Now dear, you must be strong for your father.

Stop crying," are common. Often it's not even okay to express your grief at your own mother's funeral! People who don't know how to deal with their own emotions are uncomfortable with anyone else's. Many people start putting on weight after someone in their life dies.

D. RELATIONSHIP PROBLEMS

1. Insecure spouse - codependency
   Perhaps you have an insecure spouse or relative in your home. It is important to recognize this because they can unknowingly hold you back. You may be trying to rescue this person by failing. An example is a husband who may have married a heavy woman because subconsciously he thinks no one else would want her. As she starts to lose weight, he becomes more and more insecure. He will make comments like, "Who are you losing this weight for?" Or he may begin to sabotage her by bringing home ice cream and candy.
   Many women will subconsciously defeat themselves so that their husbands can feel secure. This is not the answer. The answer is to confront them and the issue of their insecurity. Let them know that you will no longer play the game of rescuing them. Perhaps this spouse may need some self-esteem counseling to get to the bottom of his problem.

2. Disappointed expectations
   When a woman first gets married, her husband may seem like a "knight in shining armor." He rides up on his "big white stallion" and carries her off to the magic kingdom. She thinks all her dreams are coming true. But after several years and a few children later, her dreams may begin to fade away.
   One of the problems in relationships can be romance or the lack of it. Women grow up reading romance novels and continue to do so for much of their adult lives. Most men on the other hand never read romance novels. Men grow up reading sports and car magazines and of course the usual pornography.

So while girls are learning about romance and making love, men are learning about "sex." This creates very different expectations when it comes to marriage. There is a saying that "men give love to get sex and women give sex to get love." This may be true for many couples.

3. Lack of sexual fulfillment

Now you may be wondering how this affects your eating. There are several ways. Many times a husband may come home, grunt a greeting, hide behind the newspaper, and fall asleep on the couch. Then when it's bedtime he wants "sex." The woman may be needing closeness, and touching, and a few romantic words. After a while, this situation makes her feel lonely and depressed or unfulfilled. So she may begin to feel empty and turn to food to fill up that emptiness or to take away the pain. She may use food to "get fat" because subconsciously she thinks perhaps he won't want her anymore. Or she may be using food to "stuff down" unhappy feelings about her marriage she doesn't want to face up to.

Of course, we cannot generalize about all men and all women. There are many men who are romantic, and who are very considerate, sensitive lovers. And there are woman who are just as cold and unresponsive as the man described above. The point is that you need to take a look at the underlying reasons why you may be eating, and an unfulfilling relationship may be one of those.

If you want to release weight, you cannot use food to push down your emotions. You may need to start confronting your feelings about your relationship. This does not necessarily mean divorce. The first step is to see a counselor or hypnotherapist and begin to openly deal with your feelings. If you are holding back a lot of anger and resentment, you must learn to express these feelings in a healthy, nondestructive way. Yelling into a pillow or pounding on your bed are good constructive ways of releasing pent-up emotions.

The problem with most compulsive eaters is that they have been using food to "stuff" their feelings for so long, they are not even aware that they have emotions. That is what Week 3 is going to teach you. Through hypnosis you will learn to identify your emotions, which is the first step in expressing them.

Through the hypnosis and the Week 3 class, you may begin to realize that you have a pattern of emotional eating. If so, do not hesitate to ask your therapist for private hypnotherapy. This is often required to change long-term emotional eating patterns.

E. MAGIC NUMBERS

You may find yourself reaching a plateau, a certain weight which you can't seem to get below. You need to then ask yourself what getting down below that number means to you. Certain weights mean certain things to certain people.

An example was a woman who could not get below 145 pounds. Every time she started to drop below that number, she began eating everything in sight. When asked what getting below that number meant to her, she replied that it meant being attractive and sexy.

In exploring her feelings about being sexy and attractive, we learned that she had some fears about having an affair, or men pursuing her when she was "sexy and attractive." The source of this problem was revealed through hypnosis. She went back to being eleven years old and being sexually molested by her mother's new husband - her stepfather. When she told her mother, her reply was devastating: "If you hadn't been so attractive and sexy this never would have happened!" The mother divorced him, but always blamed the girl for the loss of her marriage.

So subconsciously to her being sexy and attractive meant a ruined marriage and unwanted sexual advances. When she was able to see the source of this fear and realize that it was no longer valid, she was able to get down below 145 pounds. She always knew that she had been molested, but she never made the connection between that and not being able to reach her goal weight.

The subconscious mind often makes "decisions" without

consulting the conscious mind. Because the subconscious mind is like a computer, the old "data" is still in the program until you go in and change it. This week you will be learning how to identify the old "data" that may be still affecting you from childhood decisions, or even from adult decisions that are no longer appropriate or healthy.

WEEK 3 AWARENESS EXERCISES

Emotional eating

1. What emotions trigger eating for you? Answer this question each time after doing your Week 3 tape and after the Week 3 class.

a. anger	f. emptiness	k. shame
b. fear	g. feeling deprived	l. other
c. loneliness	h. feeling rejected	
d. helplessness	i. abandonment	
e. restlessness (boredom)	j. grief	

2. Describe the emotions and how you experience them in your body, for example, tightness in your chest or stomach, etc.

_____

_____

_____

3. Describe the "scene" you went back to. How old you were, how you felt about yourself, and what messages you got from those around you. Were you taught to use food to "stuff" your emotions?

_____

_____

_____

4. How did you feel about "the child"? Are you able to love him or her? Describe your feelings about the child within you.

_____

_____

_____

5. Write out the affirmations you need to reprogram the old messages. Put them on 3 x 5 cards and repeat 25 times daily.

_____

_____

_____

Magic numbers

1. What does getting to your goal weight mean to you?

_____

_____

_____

_____

2. What were you feeling the last time in your life that you weighed this?

_____

_____

_____

_____

3. What are your fears about getting to this weight?

_____

_____

_____

_____

4. Make an affirmation to relieve this fear.

_____

_____

_____

_____

Insecure spouse
(or friend, roommate, mother, sister, neighbor, etc.)

1. List the ways that this person tries to sabotage you.

_____

_____

_____

2. What are some of the habits you believe this person needs to change and isn't?

_____

_____

_____

3. List the behaviors that tell you this person is insecure.

_____

_____

_____

4. Write some affirmations which indicate that you are taking control of your life and will no longer allow other people's insecurities to control you, e.g., "My power comes from within."

_____

_____

_____

_____

_____

_____

WEEK 4

DO YOU HANDLE STRESS BY EATING?

I. HOW YOU CREATE STRESS

There are many types of stress we all experience in our lives. The three main types are environmental, body stress, and emotional stress. We will talk about each one and how they may affect you. The important point is not how much stress you have but how you handle it. Not all people get sick when "the flu" is going around, and not all people get stressed in stressful situations. Some people thrive on stress. Why?

A. THE VICTIM SYNDROME: "THEY'RE DOIN' IT TO ME"

There are two ways to see the world in terms of who is in control of your life: either you are in control or "they" are in control. If you feel in control of your life, then the chances are that you see life as a challenge. You can take the stresses and turn them into a learning situation. If you feel helpless in your life, then you have learned "the victim" psychology and feel that "they" are doing it to you. Read *Breaking Free from the Victim Trap* for a detailed account of these ideas.

1. "Poor me"

The victim psychology is learned in families and is passed on from generation to generation. It is the attitude of "Poor me, look at how hard I try and no one appreciates me." There are many versions of the "poor me" attitude, but underlying it are some consistent qualities. It is very important to recognize if you are playing this game, so look carefully at yourself: victims come in all shapes, colors, socio-economic groups, and professions.

2. The blame game
   Besides "poor me," the victim can be most easily recognized through the "blame game." "If it weren't for you," is the common cry of the victim. "If it weren't for the boss, the weather, the economy, the customers, etc., then I could have . . ." This is a vicious cycle, because by putting the blame on others, the victim is giving away his or her power and perpetuates the feeling of helplessness.

3. The rescuer (the martyr)
   Another aspect of this game is "the martyr." The martyr "takes on" responsibility for everyone else's problems, but in the process loses responsibility for themselves. The martyr confuses love with pity and goes around trying to "rescue" the world. The martyr has an underlying belief system which says that it is good to suffer, that suffering is the way to be a "good person" and that you will surely get to heaven if you suffer enough. This of course is an outdated and ridiculous concept!

4. The victim triangle - creating stress in your life
   Now, you may be wondering how the victim and the martyr affect your stress level and your eating. The victim creates stress in an unconscious attempt to fuel the "poor me" game. The victim continues to focus on all his or her "burdens" and will create even more burdens to get even more sympathy. Remember, the victim as well as the martyr confuses love with pity. So the more pity they get, the more they feel loved.
   The martyr creates stress by taking on everyone else's problems as their own. They call it "helping," but it actually is stress they create in order to suffer so they can get their ticket to heaven! Rescuing is different from helping. When you truly care about someone else you are there to support them in solving their own problems. When you are rescuing someone else, you are taking the problem as your own. This deprives the other person of control of their own life.

The victim

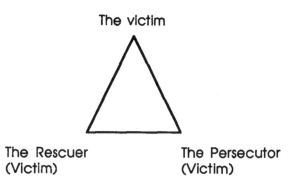

The Rescuer   The Persecutor
(Victim)   (Victim)

This is the "victim triangle." It shows how victims and rescuers interact with each other. The victim feels helpless and out of control. The rescuer will take on the victim's problems and try to rescue him or her. This makes the victim feel even more helpless, and so he/she will drop down to the role of persecutor and begin to persecute the rescuer. This makes the rescuer feel like a victim and so he/she jumps up to the victim position. It is a cycle which goes round and round and causes incredible stress in families and in the workplace. Many compulsive eaters then turn to food to handle the stress.

B. HOW CAN I STOP PLAYING THIS GAME?

1. Awareness

The first way to stop this game is to begin to recognize it in yourself and in others. Begin to notice if what you are saying could be changed to "poor me," or if you feel sorry for yourself and blame things on others. See if what you hear yourself saying could be translated into, "If it weren't for . . . , then I could have . . ." Or if you are feeling persecuted: "Why are you doing this to me?"

If you seem to have a lot of victims in your life, then you may be a rescuer and you are attracting people whose lives are falling apart. We always attract to us whatever our predominant thoughts and beliefs are. So if we are needing to feel powerful by "rescuing" others, we will attract many victims. If we are feeling helpless and playing "poor me," we will attract a lot of "rescuers" who want to help. If you feel guilty, you will attract persecutors.

The reason rescuing is unhealthy is that you are taking responsibility for someone else's problems. When you do that, you are robbing them of the opportunity to take responsibility for their own lives. You are also causing yourself so much stress, you begin to feel helpless in your own life. The way to change all this is to stop taking responsibility for others, and begin taking it for yourself.

2. Taking control of your life

You have shown that you want to take control of your life because you entered this program. Feeling out of control with food, drugs, alcohol, or tobacco is just a symptom of feeling out of control in the rest of your life. As you begin taking control of your eating, you will also begin to take control of other areas of your life. In that way you are changing the victim pattern.

3. "Thought-stopping"

Also recommended is a "thought-stopping" technique called "thumping your knuckles." Every time a negative "poor me" or victim thought comes to you, just thump your knuckle or flick it the way you do to flick off a bug. Do it several times and replace the victim thought with its opposite. If the thought is, "I do all this work and no one ever appreciates me (poor me)," then flick your knuckle and change the thought to, "I am greatly appreciated."

4. Positive affirmations

This leads us into positive affirmations. When you first say the affirmation, it may feel like a lie to you. That's okay. It is very important to realize that your thoughts create your reality. If you keep sending out the thought that no one appreciates you, it is like sending a command to those around you. They will pick up this command and stop appreciating you. By changing your negative thoughts to positive ones, you will change your reality.

Helplessness is learned and therefore it can be unlearned or changed. Consider that your mind is just like a garden. The negative thoughts are the weeds and the positive thoughts are the flowers. You need to "weed out" the negative thoughts so they don't take over and smother the positive thoughts. Also, remember that weeds grow without much encouragement and flowers need to be planted. Thought-stopping is the technique to "weed out," and affirmations the technique to "plant."

This all relates to stress because it is not how much stress you may have in your life, it is how you handle that stress. When you take control, then you find that the stress greatly diminishes. The helpless victim feelings are what cause you to feel great amounts of stress.

There have been numerous studies done on stress and helplessness. One concerned factory workers and their stress levels. They provided half of the workers with a button which they told them gave them "control" of their line. This button could stop the assembly line anytime they needed to; the other workers had no such control. They found that the workers who had the button to push had far fewer stress symptoms than the ones who felt totally helpless over their environment.

C. SOURCES OF STRESS: MENTAL AND EMOTIONAL

Many people feel work stress such as time pressures, deadlines, or difficult associates. Begin to look at these situations and see how you can take more control. There are usually ways to change things. If you can't change the situation, you can certainly change your attitude. Some individual hypnotherapy sessions will be of great value to you here.

1. "Who irritates who?"

Dealing with people who irritate you can be one of the biggest sources of stress on the job. It is important to write down the "qualities" that person seems to have. As you look at these qualities, begin to ask yourself, "Who does this person remind me of?" Many times it will be someone in your own life, like mother or father with whom you have unfinished business. In other words, you have some work to do on yourself and your relationships. Again hypnotherapy would be indicated to help you resolve these personal relationships. You can't change the other person, but you can change how you react to them.

2. Relationship stress

The relationship stress may not be at work, but instead at home. In Week 3 we talked about the insecure spouse. If you are having stress in your relationship, it must be dealt with. Many people turn to food instead of directly confronting an unhappy relationship. It is an unhealthy way of "numbing" yourself to the pain.

3. "Walking on eggshells"

Family members can be very volatile. A parent, for example, who is controlling, demanding, and critical may be a perfectionist who is always demanding that everything be his way - the only right way. The rest of the family "walks around on eggshells" trying not to set him off. This situation causes great fear and tension in everyone in the family. This type of person must be dealt with and the family stress reduced. Hypnotherapy and marriage counseling would be indicated.

4. Perfectionism

Perfectionism is a great source of mental stress for everyone in the family. The perfectionist is the person who always focuses on what hasn't been done. If you clean the house, the perfectionist will come home and focus on the cobweb you missed. If a child cleans his room, the perfectionist will get upset about the shoes he forgot to put away. So instead of giving praise, the perfectionist gives criticism.

This causes the opposite of what the perfectionist wants. He wants people to try harder, and in his presence people usually give up. A child or wife begins to feel that no matter how hard they try, nothing will please him. And they are correct, because he is always looking for something they did wrong instead of what they did right. A perfectionist in the home causes low self-esteem for everyone there.

If you see perfectionist tendencies in yourself, it would be advisable for you to immediately enter into private therapy to change this destructive behavior pattern. You are causing undue stress and emotional damage to yourself as well as your family. As you begin to change this attitude, everyone around you will become much more relaxed, their self-esteem will grow, and they will be able to perform better.

5. Worried thoughts

Another mental stress is worrying. Worrying is a destructive habit which causes stress in the body. Every time a worried thought goes through your mind, a corresponding tension is experienced physically. So if you sit and worry about money, you may begin to feel tightness in your stomach which could turn into colitis or stomach ulcers. If you sit around worrying about how fat you are, that pain in your stomach could be interpreted as hunger and may actually cause you to eat more.

Worrying is learned; children imitate what they observe in their parents. Our parents taught us to worry, and we have been teaching it to our children. Worrying is NOT problem solving and brings nothing but harmful stress reactions. It is the way you create your own stress!

There are several ways to stop worrying. You should use the "thought-stopping" technique of flicking your wrist. As you flick your wrist say to yourself, "Stop, I don't need it, and I don't want it!" Then replace the worrying thoughts with positive affirmations. A good one for money fears or any fears about lack is, "There's always plenty." Create positive affirmations because they are just as powerful as negative ones. Your thoughts create your reality; positive thoughts will change the way you handle stress and alleviate the stress you have been creating!

6. Repressing emotions

Holding in emotions can also cause stress in your body. Many physical illnesses are the result of trying to suppress feelings. Some common illnesses of suppression are: asthma, colitis, ulcers, TMJ, cancer, headaches, insomnia, chronic bronchitis, and high blood pressure. It is now estimated that 95 percent of all illnesses are caused by emotions and/or stress which is not dealt with properly.

When a person suppresses feelings, it is very common for their breathing to be difficult. The reason is that through the breath, the emotions are either expressed or suppressed. The more shallow your breathing, the more likely it is that you are suppressing feelings. Smokers use cigarettes to suppress their breathing and their emotions. Asthma is usually fear and anger held in. Tension in the jaw, or TMJ, is almost always anger; it is suppressed rage that needs to be yelled out.

An excellent way to express these emotions is through hypnotherapy. With a good therapist, you can learn how to express emotions in a safe and healthy manner. It is especially helpful to go back in age regression to times when, as a child, you were helpless and could not express what you felt, and to reclaim your personal power by saying it in the safety of the therapy session.

D. HOW TO REDUCE YOUR STRESS

1. Pillow-yelling

We teach people in our classes to yell into pillows. This is a good way to express your feelings without hurting anyone else. When you feel like eating and you are not really hungry, just sit down and write out some of your feelings. If those feelings contain some frustration, anger or resentment, go lie on your bed and do some deep breathing. Then grab your pillow and yell all the resentments into it. If you can't think of a resentment, just yell, "Get out of my body!" referring to the stress or the emotions you are holding in.

2. Hypnosis

You have already learned several significant ways to reduce

your stress in this program. The most important is relaxation. You now have a tool that you can use any time of the day or night to relax. You can use your tapes or your "thumb-and-forefinger" technique for instant relaxation. This is yours forever.

3. Deep breathing

Deep breathing is another method of relaxation. You can just sit and close your eyes and take in several long deep breaths. Or you can lie down on your bed and do connected breathing through your mouth.

4. Physical exercise

We have emphasized the importance of daily physical exercise. This practice is one of the best forms of stress reduction possible. When you exercise, your body produces serotonin, nature's relaxation hormone. You can go for a brisk walk and notice your stress being reduced in a matter of minutes. Exercise also increases your breathing, so you are actually incorporating two methods of stress reduction.

5. Nutrition

Because your nutrition is improved, you are no longer destroying the vitamins your body needs. Caffeine, sugar, alcohol, and tobacco actually destroy the B and C vitamins you need to handle stress. Eating more nutritious food and retaining the vitamin content will help you to greatly reduce your stress.

6. Individual hypnotherapy

It is important to reduce your stress by participating in hypnotherapy or counseling if you need it. Family problems or emotional problems do not go away. And if through this program you are beginning to realize that you have been eating to suppress feelings, then therapy will be a very important process for you. Dealing with your problems means that you are taking control of your life. And by taking control, you will find that you greatly reduce your stress.

II. SETTING GOALS WITH CREATIVE VISUALIZATION

A. EFFECTIVE GOAL-SETTING

Learning to set goals is one of the most effective ways to get where you are going. The subconscious mind is like a missile; it shoots straight for its target. So the important thing is to know what your goals are, and then "set" them clearly in your mind. Here are some important techniques to make goal-setting work efficiently.

1. Be specific
Be very specific about your goals. For example, with an exercise goal be sure to include the time of the day, for how long, and where you will exercise. The more detail you can supply, the more the subconscious mind will grab onto it.
EXAMPLE: "Each morning at 6:00 a.m. I ride my bicycle on the bike path for 45 minutes."

2. Positive affirmations
Make your goals into positive affirmation statements in the present tense. State it as if it is now happening.
EXAMPLE: "I weigh 135 pounds. This week I am losing 3 pounds."

3. Visualize goals
As you make your positive affirmation statement, visualize it happening. Not all people visualize - that's okay. If you don't visualize, then just imagine or use your senses and "feel" your goal happening.

4. Write it out
Each week, write your affirmations down on 3 x 5 cards and put them up all over your world. Repeat them over and over again in order to establish them strongly in the subconscious.

5. Break them down
   Set goals in each specific area of this program.
   a. Weight release goal
   b. Exercise goal
   c. Nutrition goal
   d. Eating habit goal
   e. Tape listening goal

III. THE PROGRAM IS NOW BEGINNING FOR YOU!

This is not the end of the program, but the beginning. You now have all the tools you need to reach your goal. It is just like building a house; you may have the tools, but if you don't use them the house doesn't get built. Each week we have been programming new habits into your life. New habits are beginning to take place and you can feel the changes. The entire program works as a whole.

A. PHYSIOLOGICAL CHANGES

The physiological changes we are making are:
   1. Reducing stress
   2. Evening out blood-sugar levels
   3. Controlling hormones
   4. Changing the metabolism

B. THE HABITS

The habits that have been programmed to make the above changes are:
   1. Eliminating sugar, caffeine, and alcohol
   2. Doing daily exercise
   3. Taking vitamin supplements
   4. Eating nutritious food
   5. Doing daily relaxation (hypnosis tapes or CDs)
   6. Expressing emotions in a healthy way

It all works together! These are the tools that take you to your goal. You must use them consistently for the weight to come off consistently. Each week, you may now attend a support group for one hour. This support group will help you to feel connected to others who are doing the program. It also helps you to stay on the positive track.

How to Make the Physiological Changes
Necessary to Release Weight

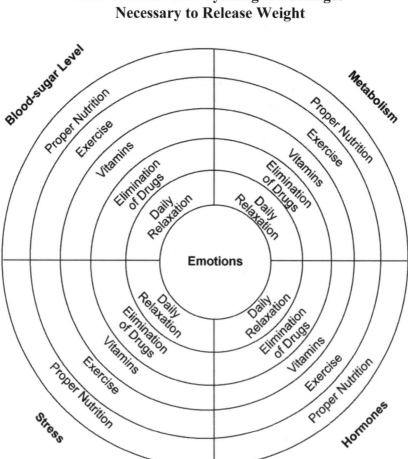

WEEK 4 AWARENESS EXERCISES

Check off the signs of stress which you had before the program and see how many have been alleviated since you've been doing the program.

Signs of stress before program   no longer have

- ❏ insomnia   ❏
- ❏ headaches   ❏
- ❏ frequent illness   ❏
- ❏ ulcers   ❏
- ❏ asthma   ❏
- ❏ nail biting   ❏
- ❏ too much alcohol   ❏
- ❏ too much tobacco   ❏
- ❏ too much food   ❏
- ❏ too much sugar   ❏
- ❏ allergies   ❏
- ❏ yelling at the kids   ❏
- ❏ other: _____   ❏
- ❏ other: _____   ❏
- ❏ other: _____   ❏

SOURCES OF STRESS IN MY LIFE

Write out:

How I feel about my job

_____

_____

_____

How I feel about my boss

_____

_____

_____

How I feel about my spouse

_____

_____

_____

How I feel about my kids

_____

_____

_____

How I feel about _____

_____

_____

_____

Now take a look at your answers and see if you are playing "the victim":

1. Could you substitute the words "poor me" for a lot of what you wrote?
2. Are you blaming others for your problems or unhappiness?
3. Could you substitute "If it weren't for you" for what you said?
4. Does it sound like, "They're doin' it to me"?
5. Is the theme, "It's not fair"?

HOW I CAN CHANGE THINGS SO THAT I'M THE WINNER, NOT THE VICTIM

1. I can change my attitude or take control in my job by

_____

_____

2. I can change my attitude or take control with my boss by

_____

_____

3. I can change my attitude or take control with my spouse by

_____

_____

4. I can change my attitude or take control with my children by

_____

_____

5. I can change my attitude or take control with _____ by

_____

_____

LIST ALL THE PEOPLE IN YOUR LIFE THAT YOU RESCUE (take on the burdens of their life). Write out how you do it.

1. _____

2. _____

3. _____

4._____

5._____

6. _____

Now write out how you are going to STOP RESCUING in each situation and write an affirmation for each one. An example of an affirmation would be: "I now give Johnnie back full responsibility for his life."

1. _____

2. _____

3. _____

4._____

5._____

6. _____

The following techniques work the best for reducing my stress:

1. Relaxation tapes or CDs

2. Daily exercise

3. Taking vitamins

4. "Calm and relaxed"

5. Individual hypnotherapy sessions

6. Taking a bath or hot tub

7. Writing out my feelings

8. Yelling into my pillow

9. "Thought-stopping"

10. Positive affirmations

**Write out all your worried thoughts and then the positive
affirmations to change them.**

1. Worried Thought: _____

Affirmation: _____

_____

2. Worried Thought: _____

Affirmation: _____

_____

3. Worried Thought: _____

Affirmation: _____

_____

4. Worried Thought: _____

Affirmation: _____

_____

5. Worried Thought: _____

Affirmation: _____

_____

MY GOALS FOR THIS PROGRAM ARE
(write out your goals as affirmations):

1. Weight release goals _____

_____

2. Nutrition goals _____

_____

3. Exercise goals _____

_____

4. Stress-reduction goals _____

_____

5. Health goals _____

_____

6. Family goals _____

_____

7. Recreation goals _____

_____

8. Counseling or hypnotherapy goals _____

_____

9. Financial goals _____

_____

10. Other _____

_____

SOME OF THE REASONS I FEEL I OR MY FAMILY NEED
INDIVIDUAL HYPNOTHERAPY:

1. _____

2. _____

3. _____

4. _____

I NO LONGER USE FOOD AS A RECREATION. NOW MY
RECREATION IS:

1. _____

2. _____

3. _____

4. _____

THE BEST THING I HAVE LEARNED FROM THIS
PROGRAM IS:

1. _____

2. _____

3. _____

4. _____

APPENDIX 1

COMMON QUESTIONS ABOUT THE TAPES OR CDs

Q. *How often should I listen to the tapes or CDs?*

A. At least once per day; more often if you wish.

Q. *What if I fall asleep when I listen?*

A. If you hear the wake-up from one to five, then you were not asleep, just in a deep state of relaxation. If you sleep through it and wake up in the morning or hours later, then you may:

1. Give yourself the suggestion before doing your tape or CD that you will hear the whole program and stay conscious.
2. Fast-forward the tape or CD past going down the stairs so that you don't go quite as deep.
3. Sit up in a chair rather than lie down on the bed.
4. Do the tape or CD at some time other than just before bed. If you like listening to your program just before bed, then do it some other time in the day also.
5. Constant heavy sleep during the tapes may be an indication that you are avoiding the program because some part of you does not want to lose weight. If you sense or feel that this may be true for you, then you may want to have a private session to uncover the reasons.

Q. *Can I play these tapes for friends or other family members?*

A. We recommend that you <u>do not</u> play these tapes or CDs for anyone else and they are not to be duplicated. They are part of a total system and should not be used by anyone who has not been through the TRIM-LIFE class.

Q. *How can I block out noise and other distractions?*

A. We recommend using headphones.

Q. *What should I eat?*

A. We don't like to tell you what you should and should not eat. Remember, this is not a diet and we do not want you to ever feel deprived. Some recipes and a few suggestions are included, however, in Appendix 4.

APPENDIX 2

THE RESEARCH

Hypnotherapy can be very helpful in making the lifestyle changes necessary for releasing weight. Examples are assessing one's physical hunger level as opposed to their "emotional" hunger level, and finding the motivation to exercise.

Hypnosis helps people identify events and memories that underlie behavior patterns that sabotage weight control. Events in daily life can trigger emotional and physical responses linked to similar events that happened years before. While hypnotized, clients are assisted to identify previous memories and responses that affect their eating and lifestyle patterns. The hypnotherapist can then help a client separate the memory from learned, inappropriate, or unhealthy behavior. Awareness allows clients to create new, more constructive habits. The reason hypnotherapy is so effective is simple: the subconscious mind is like a computer. All the memories, self-sabotage and habit control centers are located in the subconscious mind, which is akin to a multi-mega bite memory chip in your computer. Hypnosis allows access to these "internal" programs and thus the ability to make changes at the deepest level of learned habits ("programming").

Binge eating frequently is related to emotional factors, including stress reactions and mood disorders (Wegner et al., 2002). In one study, women who were categorized as binge eaters were more likely to binge on high stress days (Freeman & Gil, 2004). Binge eaters also report that they are likely to have a negative mood during days of binging, including increased feelings of anger, depression, guilt, and lowered self-image (Wegner et al., 2002). Anbar and Savedoff (2005/2006) summarize their research: "Patients with eating disorders may be **especially successful with hypnosis** because of the psychopathological origin of their symptoms (Mantle, 2003; Torem, 1992)." Eating disorders include compulsive overeating, which describes the emotional eating patterns that we address with the TRIM-LIFE PROGRAM and individual Heart-Centered Hypnotherapy sessions.

According to an analysis of weight loss treatments by Irving Kirsch (1996), the addition of **hypnosis can more than double the success rates** of cognitive-behavioral treatment. The data also indicate that the impact of hypnosis increases over time, suggesting that it is **especially useful for long-term maintenance of weight loss**.

Joseph Green (1999) summarizes the components of an effective weight loss treatment program:

(1) **Education** of medical risk factors and the dynamics of over-eating; TRIM-LIFE educates people in each weekly class as well as through the book.

(2) **Motivation** because weight loss demands self-regulation (including self-monitoring, self-evaluation, and self-reinforcement). TRIM-LIFE provides audiotapes or CDs to increase motivation.

(3) **Social support** through informing others and enlisting their agreement to not collude. TRIM-LIFE provides social support because it is accomplished in groups. The licensed therapist who runs the group, makes it safe for members to share and thus create group rapport. Through this deep sharing, we find that the members become friends and support each other through exercising together, phone calls and e-mail reminders.

(4) **Reframing urges** to eat (retraining the body to "expect" healthier foods and to "anticipate" a regular regimen of exercise). TRIM-LIFE actually uses classic "reframing" techniques to help you make healthier choices with food. We also "extinguish the urges" for foods which trigger binges.

(5) **Goal reminders** of the reasons to lose weight, including the use of affirmations and visualization. TRIM-LIFE uses these affirmations and visualization in a powerful combination, reinforced daily on the audiotapes and CDs.

(6) **Identifying triggers**, increasing control of habitual response, and increasing cues to eat less. TRIM-LIFE does this in the Week Three program where we identify the emotions which trigger binges.

(7) **Self-monitoring** habitual reaction and thus increasing conscious choice. TRIM-LIFE provides exercises at the end of each chapter to keep track of behaviors and behavior change.

(8) **Exercise** to increase energy expenditure. TRIM-LIFE provides motivation for exercise during Week Two. This motivation is reinforced through playing the audiotapes or CDs.

(9) **Hypnosis** to facilitate each of these elements. TRIM-LIFE uses hypnosis each week for all of these purposes. The audiotapes and CDs for each week contain hypnosis reinforcement sessions.

(10) **Relapse prevention** to keep from regaining the weight lost through the program, through maintaining the new healthy life-style. TRIM-LIFE accomplishes this through continued use of audiotapes or CDs and attendance of on-going support sessions.

In conclusion, we have found that the TRIM-LIFE PROGRAM includes all the ingredients of an effective weight release program as validated by research. Motivation, identifying emotional triggers, education, social support and hypnosis, all prime ingredients of this program, combine as the most successful tools in weight loss. Be sure to use all the tools in this program in order to receive the highest value.

References

Anbar, R. D., & Savedoff, A. D. (Oct 2005/Jan 2006). Treatment of binge eating with automatic word processing and self-hypnosis: A case report. *American Journal of Clinical Hypnosis*, 48(2-3), 191-198.

Freeman, L. M., & Gil, K. M. (2004). Daily stress, coping, and dietary restraint in binge eating. *The International Journal of Eating Disorders*, 36, 204-212.

Green, J. P. (1999). Hypnosis and the treatment of smoking cessation and weight loss. In I. Kirsch, A. Capafons, E. Cardeña-Buelna, & S. Amigó (Eds.), *Clinical Hypnosis and Self-Regulation: Cognitive-Behavioral Perspectives, Dissociation, Trauma, Memory, and Hypnosis Book Series*, 249-276. Washington DC: American Psychological Association.

Kirsch, I. (1996). Hypnotic enhancement of cognitive-behavioral weight loss treatments: Another meta-reanalysis. *Journal of Consulting and Clinical Psychology*, 64(3), 517-519.

Mantle, F. (2003). Eating disorders: the role of hypnosis. *Pediatric Nursing*, 15, 42-45

Torem, M. S. (1992). The use of hypnosis with eating disorders. *Psychiatric Medicine*, 10, 105-117.

Wegner, K. E., Smyth, J. M., Crosby, R. D., Wittrock, D., Wonderlich, S. A., & Mitchell, J. E. (2002). An evaluation of the relationship between mood and binge eating in the natural environment using ecological momentary assessment. *The International Journal of Eating Disorders*, 32(3), 352-361.

APPENDIX 3

CANDIDA: "I CAN'T SEEM TO LOSE WEIGHT AND I DON'T KNOW WHY."

It has now been discovered that many people are suffering from an infestation of yeast. These little microorganisms proliferate in your body and cause many problems. These are the yeast that cause bread to rise and fruit to ferment into alcohol. A certain amount of yeast is normal in our intestinal tract and around the mucosae of our bodies. Because of continual usage of antibiotics, birth control pills, cortisone, Prednisone, and other immunosuppressive drugs, the normal bacteria in our bodies have been destroyed and the yeast has flourished. Even if you haven't taken antibiotics directly, they are fed in large quantities to all the animals we eat. Stress can also cause the yeast to grow.

How do I know if I have Candida (yeast infection)?

SYMPTOMS
1. "Brainfog": difficulty remembering common names or words; feeling spacey or disconnected; feeling like you're in a "fishbowl" and that you have difficulty concentrating or remembering.

2. "Low Energy": feeling lethargic. Things that you used to do enthusiastically you are bored with or just don't have the energy to accomplish any more.

3. Craving carbohydrates or alcohol. Because the yeast "feed" on sugar you may start craving breads, alcohol, sweets and cheeses. You may find yourself gaining weight and having no control over your appetite. You may feel "hungry" all the time, or irritation and itching around the vagina, anus, mouth, gums, ears, nose, or throat. Yeast colonize in the mucous membranes.

4. PMS symptoms increase. Just before the period, increased progesterone in the blood produces an increase of sugar in the blood which in turn causes an increase in yeast. This causes the person to crave more sugar or carbohydrates and the vicious cycle continues. Headaches and cramps are worse with yeast.

5. Persistent coughs and allergy-like symptoms. Runny nose or chest congestion that won't go away. Antibiotics make it worse.

6. Gas and bloating. The gas is "smelly" and may even be painful. You may also experience intestinal problems like constipation or diarrhea. Some doctors may call it colitis, spastic colon, or "irritable bowel syndrome." Just like in baking bread, when you add sugar to yeast it expands and grows. It gets worse with sugar!

7. Symptoms increase on wet, muggy days or in the spring during the rainy season. Dampness is the breeding ground of yeast!

8. Body odors that won't go away with washing - smelly feet, etc. Athlete's foot or cold sores may be another sign of yeast.

BLOOD TESTS CAN BE GIVEN FOR DIAGNOSIS
(These tests, available from Naturopathic doctors,
are not always accurate.)

1. Candida antibody test

2. Antigen test

3. Candi-Sphere Enzyme Immuno Assay Test (CEIA)

TREATMENT FOR CANDIDA
From the book *Candida: the Epidemic of the Century Solved*
by Dr. Luc De Schepper

Treatment consists of the following principles:
1. Starve the candida (through proper diet)
2. Kill the candida (Caprylic Acid, Chinese herbs, garlic)
3. Eliminate the dead candida or toxins (enemas, colonics)
4. Avoid spreading to the blood stream (Biotin)
5. Replace the normal flora in the intestine (Acidophilus and Bifidus Bacteria, plain yogurt with no sugar)
6. Boost the natural immune system (vitamins and garlic)
7. Avoid antibiotics, hormones, and cortisone drugs if possible

I. The Candida Diet (to starve the candida)
   FOODS TO AVOID
   1. Breads
   2. Cheese and dairy products
   3. Alcohol, especially BEER
   4. Vinegar - be aware of salad dressings or condiments
   5. Foods containing SUGAR candy, cookies, ice cream, cereal, jam
   6. Mushrooms (fungus)
   7. Salad dressings which contain sugar and vinegar
   8. Greasy fried foods or "fast foods"
   9. Coffee
   10. Dried fruit and fruit juice
   11. READ LABELS. No sugar, honey, molasses, corn syrup, maple syrup, fructose, lactose, dextrose, glucose, or sucrose. Avoid canned or packaged foods, as most contain some sugar.

FOODS TO EAT

1. Rice cakes, brown rice, wild rice, buckwheat, millet, amaranth, rice noodles
2. All seafood
3. All vegetables (steamed or baked)
4. Fresh vegetable salads (lemon and cold pressed oil for dressing)
5. Fresh chicken and turkey minus skin and fat
6. Avocados and tomatoes
7. Fruits are slowly introduced after the third week. If, however, you feel the need for fruit, eat 1/2 banana. Fruits do contain fructose, so eat them with caution and watch to see if any symptoms return.
8. Corn tortillas (heat without oil in pan or oven)
9. Cashew nuts or cashew butter, macadamia nuts, almonds (only after 2nd week)
10. Fresh lemon and cold pressed linseed oil or olive oil for salad dressing

WHAT TO DRINK

1. Lemon water (hot or iced)
2. Pau D'Arco tea

Wash all fruits and veggies in water with 1 tablespoonful of Clorox added. Soak for twenty minutes, then scrub with a vegetable brush. Rinse in water and refrigerate immediately.

Do not eat leftovers or food that has been left out, as yeast tends to grow on these foods. Keep things refrigerated!

CANDIDA ALBICANS TREATMENT
(Most items can be found in health food stores)

II. Kill the Candida (yeast) with Capricin® (300-400 mg. per capsule of Caprylic Acid or Caprinex).
   A. Therapeutic dosage: 1200 mg. (3 or 4 caps) three times per day with meals for two bottles (16 days). Then begin maintenance dosage.
   B. Maintenance dosage: 1200 mg. twice per day with meals for 6 months. If symptoms return, increase to therapeutic dosage again. Watch food intake.
   C. Cervagyn. This can be applied vaginally and/or anally to eliminate the yeast in these areas. Be sure to wash applicator in Clorox after each use. Yeast can be passed on to sex partner. It helps if both do the treatment.

III. Eliminate the dead Candida or toxins.
   A. Psyllium seeds or husks ground. Each A.M. put 1 Tbsp. of psyllium in a cup of hot water. Stir well and add 1 Tbsp. of cinnamon for flavor. Drink immediately. This cleanses the colon and intestine. It also fills you up so that you may not be hungry until noon or later!
   B. Enemas every three days to eliminate toxins. Natren also makes an applicator which you can use after the enemas to implant either the acidophilus, the Capricin, or Pau D'Arco tea.

IV. Avoid spreading to the blood stream (Biotin 5 mg. daily)

V. Replace the normal flora in the intestine.
   A. Natren's Superdophilus.
      Keep refrigerated! Therapeutic dosage: 1 tsp. upon waking in A.M. 45 minutes before eating or drinking anything. Mix in a warm glass of water. Then 1 tsp. just before bed on an empty stomach. Continue for 16 days.
   B. Maintenance dosage: 1/2 tsp. A.M. and before bed.

C. Natren's Life/Start Factor-Bifidus.

VI. Boost immune system with vitamins, garlic, and daily exercise.
Vitamins:
1. Single day multiple vitamin (no yeast)
2. B Complex 100 (no yeast), 1 – 3 times per day for increased energy
3. Vitamin C, 4000 mg. per day for no more illness
4. Vitamin E, 400 to 800 units. An anti-oxidant
5. Zinc Orotate, 50 mg. Builds the immune system
6. Beta Carotene, 25,000 units. Cancer prevention
7. Selenium, 100 mcg. Enhances the properties of Vitamin E
8. Cal-Mag, 1200 mg. of calcium, 600 mg. of magnesium
9. Liquid Garlic, 3 caps 3 times per day. Boosts immune system and kills the yeast. This also prevents cancer and much, much more!

This treatment works quickly and efficiently. After three days you will no longer be craving the carbohydrates and sugars. You will feel the fog lifting and your natural energy returning. You may experience "Die-off" symptoms such as nausea. It will pass. If it is intolerable, cut back on the caprylic acid to 2 caps 3 times per day for the first week. Then increase it again.

Get started with the treatment immediately. Consult your local Naturopath for treatment assistance or your local health food store.

CANDIDA QUESTIONNAIRE AND SCORE SHEET

This will help you to know if you have Candida Albicans. If from your score you conclude that you may have it, begin the treatment. After the first three days of the treatment, you should be feeling a lot better. The craving for sugar will subside and your energy will return. Read the book *The Yeast Connection* by Dr. William Crook. This will give you many helpful hints and help you to understand more about this condition. There are also some recipes and food suggestions in the book that will help.

SECTION A: HISTORY

	Point Score
1. Have you taken tetracyclines (Sumycin[R], Panmycin[R], Vibramycin[R], etc.) or other antibiotics for acne for 1 month (or longer)?	35
2. Have you, at any time in your life, taken other "broad spectrum" antibiotics for respiratory, urinary or other infections (for 2 mos. or longer), or in shorter courses 4 or more times in a 1-year period?	35
3. Have you taken a broad spectrum antibiotic drug[a] - even a single course?	6
4. Have you, at any time in your life, been bothered by persistent prostatitis, vaginitis or other problems affecting your reproductive organs?	25
5. Have you been pregnant	
a. 2 or more times?	5
b. 1 time?	3
6. Have you taken birth control pills	
a. For more than 2 years?	15
b. For 6 months to 2 years?	8
7. Have you taken prednisone, Decadron[R] or other cortisone-type drugs	
a. For more than 2 weeks?	15
b. For 2 weeks or less?	6

8. Does exposure to perfumes, insecticides, fabric shop odors and other chemicals provoke . . .
    a. Moderate to severe symptoms? 20
    b. Mild symptoms? 5

9. Are your symptoms worse on damp, muggy days or in moldy places? 20

10. Have you had athlete's foot, ringworm, "jock itch" or other chronic fungus infections of the skin or nails? Have such infections been . . .
    a. Severe or persistent? 20
    b. Mild to moderate? 10

11. Do you crave sugar? 10

12. Do you crave breads? 10

13. Do you crave alcoholic beverages? 10

14. Does tobacco smoke really bother you? 10

15. Have you gained 10 lbs. or more for no apparent reason? . . . 10

16. Do you feel out of control with foods? 10

Total Score, Section A ....____

---

[a] Including Keflex®, ampicillin, amoxicillin, Ceclor®, Bactrim® and Septra®. Such antibiotics kill off "good germs" while they're killing off those which cause infection.

SECTION B: MAJOR SYMPTOMS

For each of your symptoms, enter your appropriate Point Score.

If a symptom is *occasional* or *mild* . . . . score 3 points
If a symptom is *frequent* and/or *moderately severe*　　score 6 points
If a symptom is *severe* and/or *disabling* . . . . score 9 points

Add total score and record it in the box at the end of this section.

	Point Score
1. Fatigue or lethargy	_____
2. Feeling of being "drained"	_____
3. Depression	_____
4. Poor memory	_____
5. Feeling "spacy" or "unreal"	_____
6. Inability to make decisions	_____
7. Numbness, burning or tingling	_____
8. Headache	_____
9. Muscle aches	_____
10. Muscle weakness or paralysis	_____
11. Pain and/or swelling in joints	_____
12. Abdominal pain	_____
13. Constipation and/or diarrhea	_____
14. Bloating, belching or intestinal gas	_____
15. Troublesome vaginal burning, itching or discharge	_____
16. Prostatitis	_____
17. Impotence	_____
18. Loss of sexual desire or feeling	_____
19. Endometriosis or infertility	_____
20. Cramps and/or other menstrual irregularities	_____
21. Premenstrual tension	_____
22. Attacks of anxiety or crying	_____
23. Cold hands or feet and/or chilliness	_____
24. Shaking or irritable when hungry	_____

Total Score, Section B . . . . _____

SECTION C: OTHER SYMPTOMS*

For each of your symptoms, enter your appropriate Point Score.

If a symptom is *occasional* or *mild* . . . . score 1 point
If a symptom is *frequent* and/or *moderately severe*　　score 2 points
If a symptom is *severe* and/or *disabling* . . . .　score 3 points

Add total score and record it in the box at the end of this section.

		Point Score
1.	Drowsiness	____
2.	Irritability or jitteriness	____
3.	Incoordination	____
4.	Inability to concentrate	____
5.	Frequent mood swings	____
6.	Insomnia	____
7.	Dizziness/loss of balance	____
8.	Pressure above ears ... feeling of head swelling	____
9.	Tendency to bruise easily	____
10.	Chronic rashes or itching	____
11.	Numbness, tingling	____
12.	Indigestion or heartburn	____
13.	Food sensitivity or intolerance	____
14.	Mucus in stools	____
15.	Rectal itching	____
16.	Dry mouth or throat	____
17.	Rash or blisters in mouth	____
18.	Bad breath	____
19.	Foot, hair or body odor not relieved by washing	____
20.	Nasal congestion or post nasal drip	____
21.	Nasal itching	____
22.	Sore throat	____
23.	Laryngitis, loss of voice	____

---

*While the symptoms in this section commonly occur in people with yeast-connected illness, they are also found in other individuals.

24. Cough or recurrent bronchitis   _____
25. Pain or tightness in chest   _____
26. Wheezing or shortness of breath   _____
27. Urinary frequency or urgency   _____
28. Burning on urination   _____
29. Spots in front of eyes or erratic vision   _____
30. Burning or tearing of eyes   _____
31. Recurrent infections or fluid in ears   _____
32. Ear pain or deafness   _____

Total Score, Section C   _____

Total Score, Section A   _____

Total Score, Section B   _____

GRAND TOTAL SCORE _____

The Grand Total Score will help you and your physician decide if your health problems are yeast-connected. Scores in women will run higher as 7 items in the Questionnaire apply exclusively to women, while only 2 apply exclusively to men.

Yeast-connected health problems are **almost certainly** present in women with scores *over 180*, and in men with scores *over 140*.

Yeast-connected health problems are **probably** present in women with scores *over 120*, and in men with scores *over 90*.

Yeast-connected health problems are **possibly** present in women with scores *over 60*, and in men with scores *over 40*.

With scores of less than 60 in women and 40 in men, yeasts are less apt to cause health problems.

Copyright 1986, *The Yeast Connection*, pages 30-33, by William G. Crook, M.D.

APPENDIX 4

FOOD SERVING IDEAS

PROTEIN
- Red Meats
- Fish
  - Salmon   Halibut
  - Albacore   Tuna
  - Black Cod Sardines
- Fowl
  - Chicken   Turkey
- Legumes
  - Black-eyed peas
  - Black beans
  - Kidney beans
  - Pinto beans Lentils
  - Navy beans
  - Garbanzo beans
  - Legume based cold cuts
  - Lima beans
  - Soybeans
- Nuts & Seeds
  - Almond   Walnuts
  - Pistachios Soy nuts
  - Pecans   Cashews
  - Hazelnuts Seeds
  - Nut butters
- Protein Shakes & Bars
- Soy
  - Tofu   Tempeh
  - Miso   Edemame
  - Soy nuts   Soymilk
  - Soy-based cold cuts
- Eggs
- Dairy
  - Yogurt   Cheese
  - Milk
  - Cottage Cheese

VEGETABLES
- Leafy greens
  - Cabbage   Chard
  - Collards   Kale
  - Spinach   Beet greens
  - Salad greens Lettuce
- Stems
  - Asparagus, Celery, Leeks
- Roots & Tubers
  - Beets   Carrots
  - Parsnips   Garlic
  - Onions   Radishes
- Vegetable flowers
  - Broccoli   Cauliflower
  - Artichokes
  - Brussel Sprouts
- Flowering vegetables
  - Cucumbers   Eggplants
  - Peppers   Pumpkins
  - Squash   Tomatoes
  - Okra
- Seaweeds & Mushrooms
  - Nori, Kelp, Shitake

GRAINS
- Whole Grains
  - Barley   Millet
  - Rice   Oats
  - Buckwheat   Rye
  - Wheat   Quinoa

CARBOHYDRATES
Apples, Apricot, Cherries, Pears,
Grapes, Peaches, Oranges, Plums,
Grapefruit, Limes, Lemons,
Cantaloupes, Casabas, Honey dew,
Watermelons, Strawberries

HEALTHY SELECTION FROM FOOD GROUPS

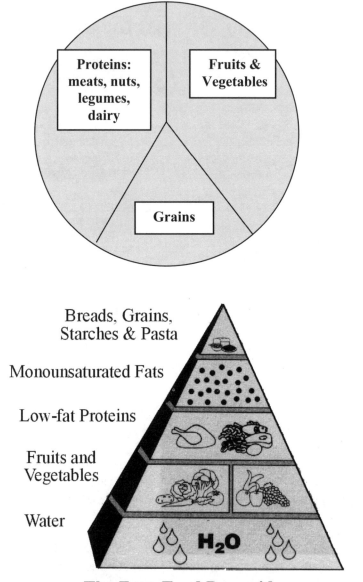

The Zone Food Pyramid
(from *Mastering the Zone*)
To help you see how to balance *healthy food choices*

CARBOHYDRATE GRAM COUNTER
(from *Dr. Atkins' New Diet Revolution*)

Food	Grams	Food	Grams
MILK, CREAM AND BUTTER		**GRAINS, BREADS AND PASTA**	
Butter (1 tsp)	0	Bagel (2 1/2 oz)	38
Half and Half (2 tbsp)	1	Biscuit (2 oz)	27.6
Heavy Whipping Cream (2 tbsp)	0.8	Blueberry Muffin (2 oz)	27.4
Milk (2%, 1 cup)	11.7	Corn Flakes (1 cup)	24.2
(whole, 1 cup)	11.4	Corn Muffin (2 oz)	29
Sour Cream (2 tbsp)	1.2	Crackers (butter-type, 5)	51.4
Yogurt (whole milk, plain, 1 cup)	11.4	English Muffin	26
		Italian Bread (1 slice)	15
CHEESE		Oatmeal (cooked 1/2 cup)	12.6
American (slice, 2/3 oz)	0.3	Pancake (6" diameter)	21.8
Bleu (crumbled, 2 tbsp)	0.4	Pasta (cooked, 1/2 cup)	19.8
Cheddar (shredded, 2 tbsp)	0.2	Pasta (whole wheat,	
Cream Cheese (2 tbsp)	0.8	(cooked, 1/2 cup)	18.6
Feta (crumbled, 2 tbsp)	0.8	Pita Pocket Bread	
Monterey Jack (2 tbsp)	0.1	(6 1/2" diameter)	33.4
Mozzarella (whole milk, 2 tbsp)	0.3	Puffed Wheat Cereal (1 cup)	11.1
Parmesan (shredded, 2 tbsp)	0.3	Basin Bran (1 cup)	47.1
Ricotta (whole milk, ' cup)	1.9	Rice (white, cooked, 1/2 cup)	22.3
Swiss (shredded, 2 tbsp)	0.5	Tortilla (corn)	12.1
		Waffle (homemade, 7" diameter)	24.7
NUTS AND SEEDS		White Bread (1 slice)	14.9
Almond Butter (2 tbsp)	6.8	Whole Grain Bread (1 slice)	11.8
Almonds (whole, 2 tbsp)	3.6		
Hazelnuts (whole, 2 tbsp)	2.8	**SOUPS**	
Macadamia (2 tbsp)	2.3	Beef Broth (1 cup)	1
Peanut Butter (natural,		Black Bean (1 cup)	19.8
no sugar added, 2 tbsp)	6.9	Chicken Noodle (1 cup)	9.4
Peanuts (2 tbsp)	3.4	Cream of Tomato (1 cup)	22.3
Pecans (chopped, 2 tbsp)	2.1	Minestrone (1 cup)	11.2
Pine Nuts (2 tbsp)	2.4	Clam Chowder (1 cup)	16.6
Pistachio Nuts (2 tbsp)	4.7	Onion (1 cup)	8.2
Pumpkin Seeds (2 tbsp)	3.1		
Walnuts (2 tbsp)	1.7		

CONDIMENTS, SAUCE, HERBS

Barbecue Sauce (2 tbsp)	4
Chili Powder (1 tsp)	1.4
Cranberry Sauce (2 tbsp)	13.5
Dijon Mustard (1 tsp)	0.6
Fresh Herbs (all types, 1 tbsp)	0.1
Garlic (1 clove)	1
Ginger Root (sliced, 1 tbsp)	0.9
Gravy (canned, 1/4 cup)	3.2
Hollandaise Sauce (2 tbsp)	0.3
Honey (1 tsp)	5.8
Jam (1 tsp)	4.6
Ketchup (1 tbsp)	4.2
Maple Syrup (1 tbsp)	13.4
Olives (green, 5)	2.5
Pickle Relish (1 tbsp)	5.4
Salsa (red, 1 tbsp)	0.8
Soy Sauce (1 tbsp)	1
Marinara Sauce (1/4 cup)	5.1
Sweet & Sour Sauce (1/4 cup)	15.1
Tartar Sauce (2 tbsp)	1.2
Teriyaki Sauce (2 tbsp)	5.7
White Wine Vinegar (1 tbsp)	1.5

VEGETABLES

Artichoke (1)	13.4
Asparagus (6 spears)	3.8
Beans (green, 1/2 cup)	4.9
Broccoli (1/2 cup)	3.9
Cabbage (green, 1/2 cup)	1.9
Carrot (medium)	7.3
Cauliflower (6 florets)	4.4
Celery (1 stalk)	1.5
Collards (4 oz)	7.3
Corn (1/2 cup)	16
Cucumber (1/2 small)	2.5
Eggplant (1/2 cup)	3.3
Endive (1/2 cup)	1.8
Escarole (1/2 cup)	0.8

Jicama (1/2 cup)	5.7
Leek (1)	12.6
Lettuce (Butterhead, 1 cup)	1.3
(Romaine, 1 cup)	1.3
Mushroom (Portobello, 1/2 cup)	1.4
Okra (4 oz)	7.5
Onion (1)	9.5
Onions (green, 1/4 cup)	1.8
Peas (green, 1/2 cup)	9.9
Peppers (green, 1/2 cup)	4.8
Potato (sweet, 1)	22.4
Potato (white, 1/2 cup)	15.4
Pumpkin (1/2 cup)	9.9
Spinach (raw, 1 cup)	1.1
Squash (butternut, 1/2 cup)	10.8
Tomato (1 small)	4.2
Zucchini (1 small)	5.7

MEAT, POULTRY AND FISH

Meat, Poultry, Fish (6 oz)	0
Eggs (1)	0.6
Beef Salami (3 oz)	2.4
Calf Liver (6 oz)	10.4

SEAFOOD

Clams (canned, 6 oz)	8.7
Lobster (6 oz)	2.2
Oysters (6 oz)	12.5
Scallops (6 oz)	3.9
Shrimp (6 oz)	0
Squid (6 oz)	7

OILS AND DRESSINGS

Mayonnaise (1 tsp)	0.1
Olive Oil (1 tsp)	0
Salad Dressing (Caesar, 2 tbsp)	0.6
(Italian, 2 tbsp)	3
(Ranch, 2 tbsp)	1.4
Vegetable Oil (1 tsp)	0

BEANS

Baby Lima (1/2 cup)	21.2
Black (1/2 cup)	20.4
Chickpea/Garbanzo (1/2 cup)	22.5
Lentils (1/2 cup)	19.9
Navy (1/2 cup)	23.9
Red Kidney (1/2 cup)	19.8
Soybeans (1/2 cup)	9.9

FRUIT AND FRUIT JUICES

Apple (1 medium)	21
Applesauce (1/4 cup)	6.9
Apricots (fresh, 1)	3.9
Avocado (1)	14.9
Banana (1 small)	23.7
Blueberries (1/4 cup)	5.1
Cantaloupe (1/4 cup)	3.3
Cherries (1/4 cup)	4.8
Fig (fresh, 1)	9.6
Grapes (1/4 cup)	7.1
Honeydew (1/4 cup)	3.9
Juice, lemon (1 tbsp)	1.3
Juice, orange (1/2 cup)	13.4
Juice, tomato (1/2 cup)	5.1
Kiwifruit (1)	11.3
Mango (1/4 cup)	7
Orange (1)	16.3
Peach (1 medium)	10.9

Pear (1 medium)	25.1
Pineapple (1/4 cup)	4.8
Plum (1)	8.6
Raspberries (1/4 cup)	3.6
Strawberries (1/4 cup)	2.7
Tangerine (1)	7.8
Watermelon (1/4 cup)	2.8

HIGH-CARB *FATTENING* ITEMS

Apple Pie (1/8 of a 9" pie)	57.5
Bean Burrito	48
Beer (12 fl oz)	13.2
Cheeseburger with Bun (1/4 lb)	33
Chocolate (dark, 1 oz)	17.9
Chocolate Ice Cream (1/2 cup)	18.6
Chocolate Layer Cake (3 oz)	38
Croissant	27
Doughnut (glazed)	26.6
Egg Roll (1)	30
Hot Dog with Bun	24
Macaroni and Cheese (1 cup)	40
Milk Shake (medium)	90
Oatmeal Cookie (1/2 oz)	12.4
Onion Rings	33
Pecan Pie (1/8 of a 9" pie)	63.7
Pizza (1 slice)	24
Pretzels (10 pieces)	47.5
Tortilla Chips	11.3

The Level of Sugar in Your Blood
(from *Potatoes Not Prozac*, p. 40)

Your body uses a very simple form of sugar called glucose as its basic fuel. During digestion all the carbohydrates you eat are broken down into glucose. It is carried by the blood throughout your body to be used as energy by the cells as needed. All your cells, particularly those in your brain, require a steady supply of sugar at all times.

When your body has the optimal level of sugar in the blood to supply your cells, you feel good. When your blood sugar level is too low, your cells don't get the sugar they need and they start sending out distress signals. These distress signals are the symptoms of low blood sugar, a condition known as hypoglycemia.

Optimal Blood Sugar	Low Blood Sugar
Energetic	Tired all the time
Tired when appropriate	Tired for no reason
Focused and relaxed	Restless, can't keep still
Clear	Confused
Having a good memory	Having trouble remembering
Able to concentrate	Having trouble concentrating
Able to solve problems effectively	Easily frustrated
Easygoing	More irritable than usual
Even-tempered	Getting angry unexpectedly

Brain Chemicals: Serotonin
(from *Potatoes Not Prozac*, p. 41)

In addition to blood sugar, a number of chemicals in your brain affect how you feel and act. Serotonin is a brain chemical that is particularly important for sugar-sensitive people. It creates a sense of relaxation, "mellows you out" and gives you a sense of being at peace with the world. Serotonin also influences your self-control, impulse control and ability to plan ahead.

Optimal Level of Serotonin	Low Level of Serotonin
Hopeful, optimistic	Depressed
Reflective and thoughtful	Impulsive
Able to concentrate	Having a short attention span
Creative, focused	Blocked, scattered
Able to think things through	Flying off the handle
Able to seek help	Suicidal
Responsive	Reactive
Looking forward to dessert without an emotional charge	Craving sweets
Hungry for a variety of different foods	Craving mostly carbohydrates like bread, pasta and cereal

Foods and their Level of Tryptophan
(from *Potatoes Not Prozac*, p. 110)

Protein Food	Serving	Tryptophan (mg)
Chicken (white)	4 oz.	390
Turkey	4 oz.	390
Cheddar cheese	1 cup	330
Ground beef	4 oz.	320
Tuna	4 oz.	320
Tempeh	4 oz.	310
Cottage cheese	1 cup	300
Tofu	4 oz.	280
Salmon	4 oz.	250
Soy protein powder	1 oz. (2 Tbs.)	220
Scrambled eggs	2	200
Spaghetti, whole wheat	2 cups cooked	190
Kidney beans	1 cup	180
Quinoa (a grain)	1 cup cooked	110
Almonds	.5 cup	170
Lentils	1 cup cooked	160
Milk	8 oz.	110
Soy milk	8 oz.	110
Yogurt	8 oz.	70

Use this list as a guideline to help choose proteins with more tryptophan as you create a food plan which works for you. Animal proteins are higher in amino acids (and therefore tryptophan) than foods like milk or almonds. If you are vegetarian, quinoa and soy will give you more than enough tryptophan.

The Glycemic Index
(from *The South Beach Diet*, pp. 70-74)

The following table lists the **glycemic index** of many of the foods you're likely to encounter in your daily life. The choices are grouped by type of food, then arranged in each group from foods with the lowest glycemic index to those with the highest.

A food's glycemic index is **the amount that it increases** your **blood sugar** compared to the amount that the same quantity of white bread would increase it.

The foods with the **lower numbers** will cause your blood sugar to rise then fall **more slowly** than the foods with higher numbers will. Numerous studies have also shown that **low-glycemic foods satisfy your hunger longer** and **minimize** your food cravings better.

Even though low-fat milk and peanut M&Ms have the same glycemic index, obviously the milk is a much better nutritional choice because of the nutritional advantage. This is what <u>healthy choices</u> are about.

BAKERY PRODUCTS	GI
Sponge cake	66
Pound cake	77
Danish	84
Muffin	88
Flan	93
Angel food cake	95
Croissant	96
Doughnut	108
Waffles	109
BEVERAGES	**GI**
Soy milk	43
Apple juice (unsweetened)	57
Pineapple juice	66
Grapefruit juice	69
BREADS	**GI**
Oat bran bread	68

	GI
Mixed grain bread	69
Pumpernickel	71
White pita	82
Cheese pizza	86
Hamburger bun	87
Rye flour bread	92
Semolina bread	92
Oat kernel bread	93
Whole wheat bread	99
Melba toast	100
White bread	101
Plain Bagel	103
Kaiser rolls	104
Bread stuffing	106
Gluten-free wheat bread	129
French baguette	136

BREAKFAST CEREALS	GI
Rice bran	27
All-Bran	60
Oatmeal, noninstant	70
Special K	77
Kellogg's Smacks	78
Oat bran	78
Muesli	80
Kellogg's Mini-Wheats (whole wheat)	81
Bran Chex	83
Kellogg's Just Right	84
Life	94
Grape-Nuts	96
Shredded Wheat	99
Cream of Wheat	100
Golden Grahams	102
Puffed Wheat	105
Cheerios	106
Corn Bran	107
Total	109
Rice Krispies	117
Com Chex	118
Cornflakes	119
Crispix	124
Rice Chex	127

CEREAL GRAINS	GI
Pearled barley	36
Rye	48
Wheat kernels	59
Rice, instant	65
Bulgur	68
Rice, parboiled	68
Cracked barley	72
Wheat, quick cooking	77
Buckwheat	78
Brown rice	79
Wild rice	81
White rice	83
Couscous	93
Rolled barley	94
Mahatma Premium Rice	94
Taco shells	97
Cornmeal	98
Millet	101
Tapioca, boiled with milk	115

COOKIES	GI
Oatmeal cookies	79
Shortbread	91
Arrowroot	95
Graham crackers	106
Vanilla wafers	110
Biscotti	113

CRACKERS	GI
Breton wheat crackers	96
Stoned wheat thins	96
Rice cakes	110

DAIRY FOODS	GI
Low fat yogurt, artificially sweetened	20
Chocolate milk, artificially sweetened	34
Whole milk	39
Fat-free milk	46
Low fat yogurt, fruit flavored	47
Low-fat ice cream	71
Ice cream	87

FRUIT AND FRUIT PRODUCTS	GI
Cherries	32
Apple juice	34
Grapefruit	36
Peach	40
Dried apricots	43
Fresh apricots	43
Canned peach	43
Orange	47
Pear	47
Plum	55
Apple	56
Grapes	62
Canned pear	63
Raisins	64
Pineapple juice	66
Grapefruit juice	69
Fruit cocktail	79
Kiwifruit	83
Mango	86
Banana	89
Canned apricots, in syrup	91
Pineapple	94
Watermelon	103

LEGUMES	GI
Soybeans, boiled	23
Red lentils, boiled	36
Kidney beans, boiled	42
Green lentils, boiled	42
Butter beans, boiled	44
Yellow split peas, boiled	45
Baby lima beans, frozen	46
Chickpeas	47
Navy beans, boiled	54
Pinto beans	55
Black-eyed peas	59
Canned chickpeas	60
Canned pinto beans	64
Canned baked beans	69
Canned kidney beans	74
Canned green lentils	74

PASTA	GI
Protein-enriched spaghetti	38
Fettuccine	46
Vermicelli	50
Whole grain spaghetti	53
Meat-filled ravioli	56
White spaghetti	59
Capellini	64
Macaroni	64
Linguine	65
Cheese tortellini	71
Durum spaghetti	78
Macaroni and cheese	92
Gnocchi	95
Brown rice pasta	113

ROOT VEGETABLES	GI
Sweet potato	63
Carrots, cooked	70
Yam	73
White potato, boiled	83
Potato, steamed	93
Potato, mashed	100
New potato	101
Rutabaga	103
Potato, boiled, mashed	104
French fries	107
Potato, instant	114

Potato, microwaved	117
Parsnips	139
Potato, baked	158

SNACK FOOD & CANDY	GI
Peanuts	21
Mars M&Ms (peanut)	46
Mars Snickers Bar	57
Mars Twix Cookie Bars	62
Chocolate bar, 1.5 oz	70
Jams and marmalades	70
Potato chips	77
Popcorn	79
Mars Kudos Whole Grain Bars (chocolate chip)	87
Mars Bar	91
Mars Skittles	98
Life Savers	100
Corn chips	105
Jelly beans	114
Pretzels	116
Dates	146

SOUPS	GI
Canned tomato soup	54
Canned Lentil soup	63
Split pea soup	86
Black bean soup	92
Canned green pea soup	94

SUGARS	GI	Collard	<20
Fructose	32	Kale	<20
Lactose	65	Mustard	<20
Honey	83	Spinach	<20
High-fructose corn syrup	89	Turnip	<20
Sucrose	92	Lettuce, all varieties	<20
Glucose	137	Mushrooms, all varieties	<20
Maltodextrin	150	Okra	<20
Maltose	150	Peanuts	<20
VEGETABLES	**GI**	Peppers, all varieties	<20
Artichoke	<20	Green beans	<20
Arugula	<20	Snow peas	<20
Asparagus	<20	Spaghetti squash	<20
Broccoli	<20	Young summer squash	<20
Brussels sprouts	<20	Watercress	<20
Cabbage, all varieties	<20	Wax beans	<20
Cauliflower	<20	Zucchini	<20
Celery	<20	Tomatoes	23
Cucumbers	<20	Dried peas	32
Escarole	<20	Green peas	68
Eggplant	<20	Sweet corn	78
Beet	<20	Pumpkin	107
Chard	<20		

FOOD SERVING IDEAS

Breakfast:
- **Eggs:**
  - Hard boiled or poached eggs (ahead of time boil enough eggs for 2-3 days, and have them ready in the fridge)
  - Omelet – onions, bell peppers, mushrooms, zucchini, spinach, and cheese
  - Large Frittata or Mini Frittatas (open faced omelet in individualized cups): 6 eggs mixed with veggies, turkey sausage, spinach leaves, onions, basil leaves, sundried tomatoes, etc. [Bake 350 degrees for 15 minutes]
  - Poached eggs with Gruyere sauce on top of a thick tomato slice

- **Breakfast scramble:** beans, low-fat turkey sausage, poached egg or scrambled tofu, salsa and guacamole. Serve on a plate with melted cheese and plain yogurt.
  - You can purchase pre-cooked beans or make them from scratch.
  - A cheap and easy way to cook beans to keep them from causing gas or poor digestion (this method breaks down the disaccharides in the beans which make them difficult to digest):
  - Soak dried beans overnight or bring to a boil in water (a 1:1 ratio of beans to water) and let sit off heat for 2 hours. Discard the water, rinse, and then cook for at least 2 hours until you can mash them easily on the roof of your mouth with your tongue.
  - Add 1-2 Tablespoons of one: cumin, tumeric, paprika, or Mexican spices
  - After they are done cooking, add 1 tsp of salt per 2 cups of beans (salt softens the skins and makes them more digestible).

- **Plain yogurt** with a small handful of raw nuts and seeds mixed in add Stevia and/or Splenda for sweetener.

- **Protein bar:** look for ones low in carbohydrates. They come in chocolate, rice crispy & chocolate, peanut butter & almond flavors.

- **Protein shake/Smoothie:**
  - Frozen blueberries, strawberries, raspberries, blackberries, or other berries (1/4 to 1/2 cup).
  - 1-2 scoops of protein powder or 1 Tablespoon of nut butter.
  - 1/2 cup of rice, almond, oat or soy milk plus water to desired consistency.
  - Blend well! Can also add: psyllium seeds, 3 Tablespoons of flax oil or 1 Tablespoon of (lemon) cod liver oil and other powdered vitamins.
  - **Fiber:** Begin by adding a small amount of fiber (such as bran) and increase until you reach the ideal bowel.

Lunch & **Dinner:** *for anti-inflammatory, concentrate on deep sea fish and avoid red meats*
- Pre-made foods
  - Low carb meals - Lean Cuisine & Healthy Choice & South Beach
  - Get the deli to pre-package some meals from the Deli
- Baked or Grilled fish, chicken, turkey, tofu (with steamed or sauteed vegetables)
  - Easy options:
    - On the weekends, bake large quantities of these. The easiest to do is place several pieces on a cookie sheet and drizzle a different flavor of Annie's salad dressings over a few pieces of chicken/ fish/ turkey and bake – this way you'll end up with several different flavors of healthy and delicious protein/ main course dishes. Freeze leftovers if you won't eat them within about 4 days.
    - You can marinate in Annie's dressing or other combination of flavors:
      - Soy sauce/ Tamari with toasted sesame oil (you may also want to try brown rice vinegar or Miri or Sake as a marinade)
      - Lemon with olive oil and dried thyme and rosemary (other herbs: fresh parsley, basil, dill or oregano).
    - Olive oil, cumin and paprika.
  - Can bake plain and top with healthy sauces
    - Annie's Dressings, pesto, salsa, chutney

- **Deep sea fish:**
  - Salmon, Halibut, Sea Bass, Tuna, Cod, Mackerel, Sardines, Anchovies – they're high in omega 3's which are anti-inflammatory and lower cholesterol.
  - Try sardines canned in mustard or tomato sauces.
  - Add Anchovies to salads i.e., Caesar
  - Serve your proteins with steamed vegetables or a salad
- **Chicken breasts** stuffed with prosciuto or ham & provolone
- **Stir fry** vegetables with chicken or tofu, with favorite condiments
- **Meat Loaf:** ground chicken, ground turkey, or ground beef
- **Skewers:** chicken, beef, or fish with vegetables
- **Sandwiches** in the form of a roll up: [contents without the bread - rolled up in turkey slice; or with a low-carb bread] turkey, lettuce, tomato, Dijon mustard
- **Pasta** (also see below):
  - Noodles made out of beans (legumes) or wheat bran & germ (but no wheat flour) "Da Boles." Just when you are about to finish cooking the noodles, add broccoli or kale.
- **Quiche:** the crust can be made with a bean flour ("Red Mill" brand) such as garbanzo beans. Eggs, broccoli, onions, and spinach
- **Pizza:** ham or salami or ground chicken or ground beef & cheese - (made with "Red Mill" brand – bean flour)
- **Salads:**
  - Mixed Green Salad with vegetables added (such as purple cabbage, onions, bell peppers)
    - Add protein, such as: chicken or turkey, albacore tuna, marinated tofu, beans (chick peas & black beans), raw nuts, seeds, and sliced eggs, soy or regular low fat cheese, [salad dressing to include flax seed oil – natural anti-inflammatory]
  - Cobb Salad: mixed greens with strips of hard boiled eggs, walnuts, tomatoes & chicken or ham.
  - Pre-made tuna, chicken or egg salad with some veggies on the side (use Spectrum canola oil mayo or plain yogurt)
- **Soups & Stews:** without the noodles and tubers (potatoes, yams, sweet potatoes). Use a crock pot or slow cooker.
  - Legumes/Bean (7-bean soups with textured vegetable protein. Add some salsa and guacamole or raw onions.

- Chili with ground beef, chicken, or tempeh
- Tofu (miso) – break up an egg in the soup
- Tom Yum Soup – found at Thai restaurants
- Gumbo Soup – sausage, chicken, shrimp, with vegetables (onions, red pepper) with some cayenne
- **Marinated Tofu**
  - Marinated in vinegar and Stevia and/or Splenda, or in Annie's dressings.
- **Burrito:** [contents without the actual wrap] black beans, low fat turkey/ chicken sausage, salsa, guacamole, chicken. Use yogurt instead of sour cream.
- **Burgers:** Chicken, turkey, salmon or bean/soy [Boca] without the bun. Add soy cheese, lettuce, tomato, onion, mustard, salsa & guacamole.
- **Roll-Ups:**
  - Lettuce wrap (Butter lettuce) with some protein inside (beans/hummus, turkey or chicken slice, marinated tofu, asparagus)
  - Romaine lettuce leaf boats to serve
    - bean dips (hummus & black bean) or
    - egg, chicken or tuna salad
    - crab meat mixed with low fat cream cheese
  - Turkey slices to wrap other foods such as hummus and veggies (carrot strips, asparagus, celery sticks)
  - Cabbage leaves [if steamed you can peel the leaves off]. Wrap with kidney beans, low fat turkey sausage and mustard
- **Restaurants:**
  - "World Wraps" - served in a bowl without the wrap and rice, and extra vegetables or beans
  - Ask to hold the potato, rice, bread and pasta and ask for more vegetables instead
  - Ask for Stir Frys or salads with an extra serving of protein
- **Low-Carb breads & pasta**
  - Low-Carb bread/ tortilla are okay as long as the first ingredient is wheat germ/bran or a protein source (bean flour). Make sure wheat flour is the last ingredient.
  - Atkins makes a low-carb pasta.
  - Can make low-carb tortilla chips by baking the tortillas

Snacks:
- Cottage cheese with veggies (tomatoes. cucumbers, carrots)
- Edanome (soy beans)
- Eggs: Deviled eggs, hard boiled or poached eggs, or pickled eggs
- Turkey balls (Trader Joe's)
- Small handful of raw nuts and seeds
- Dips for raw vegetables:
  - Bean: put in a blender the following items: cooked or canned beans, garlic, lemon juice, olive oil, salt and pepper, favorite herbs, e.g., hummus
  - Crab and mushroom dip
  - Spinach and goat cheese dip
  - Hummus with black eye peas, or split peas or black beans
  - Artichoke dip
  - Guacamole
  - Nut butters (almond, cashew, hazelnut, sesame - tahini)
- Stevia and/or Splenda or xylitol sweetened gum
- Protein bars or protein shakes
- Fruits you can have - any non-sweet or low glycemic ones:
  - Cranberry, lemon, lime, grapefruit, palmello, pomegranate
  - Melons & cottage cheese
- If you're having a craving for sweets, have baker's unsweetened chocolate, (add unsweetened coconut) -- melt down and mix with Stevia and/or Splenda and mixed nuts. Put on a cookie sheet in the freezer. Add some natural extracts for flavor (almond, vanilla).
- Celery and nut butter.

Beverages:
- Water
- Iced herbal or green tea with Stevia and/or Splenda or xylitol
- Licorice root tea (tastes sweet)
- Coffee Substitutes: Caf-Lib, Raja's Cup, Roastaroma, Almond Sunrise; Stevia and/or Splenda or xylitol to sweeten
- Black tea substitute: Rooibus (red tea)
- Seltzer water (Perrier or non-flavored Talking Rain) with lemon
- Iced lemonade with Stevia and/or Splenda (try with limes, white grapefruit, or cranberries)
- Virgin Mojito (mint drink)

Condiments:
- Minced seaweed to salt foods (Nori, Dulse, Kelp powder)
- Salsa
- Guacamole
- Wheat-free tamari / Soy Sauce
- Garlic
- Onions
- Fresh herbs (cilantro, basil)
- Pesto (Costco has it in jars – great on fish or chicken)
- Lime, lemon, & grapefruit juices
- Hot peppers
- Vinegars: red wine, balsamic, apple cider
- Mustard (for sweet mustards add Stevia and/or Splenda)
- Horseradish/ Wasabe
- Taziki sauce: yogurt with cucumbers
- Tarter sauce: try Spectrum brand made with canola oil. Add dill pickles instead of relish.
- Tomato sauce - add Stevia and/or Splenda to sweeten, Italian herbs for turkey meat balls or turkey meatloaf
- Canned tomatoes
- Dressings:
  - Annie's brand dressings
  - Powdered mustard added to oil (flax seed oil) and vinegar with Stevia and/or Splenda
  - Lime, lemon or grapefruit juices added to Tahini dressings

FOOD SUGGESTIONS AND RECIPES

BREAKFASTS

7-GRAIN CEREAL
Or any hot cereal like oatmeal (not instant).
Add cinnamon; raisins, bananas, strawberries, or apples; a small
amount of Nutrasweet

FILLING FIBER CEREAL (makes enough for eight days)
  3 cups of Bran Flakes (any kind with the least sugar)
  1 1/2 cups of bran (this is the bulk kind in health food stores)
  1 1/2 cups of Bran Buds or All-Bran
  1 cup pecans or almonds, chopped
  8 large pitted prunes, chopped
  16 dried apricot halves, chopped
  1/2 cup raisins

Place all ingredients in a large bowl and gently mix with 2 forks.
Put it all into a large ziplock bag and keep it in the refrigerator. The
bran will have a tendency to go to the bottom so mix it a little when
you serve it up. It will only take a small amount of this to fill you
up! Nonfat milk goes well with this and you probably will find the
fruit is all the sweetener you need.

RICOTTA CHEESE BREAKFAST
  Mix container of ricotta cheese with
  Cinnamon to taste
  1 tsp. vanilla
  1 pkg. Equal

Spread a small amount on a slice of good whole wheat low carb
bread or a rice cake and broil for a couple of minutes - just until
brown and warm. DELICIOUS!

LUNCHES

HALF SANDWICHES
  Turkey with mustard, tomato and lettuce

Chicken with mustard, tomato and lettuce

Tuna with low-fat mayonnaise (Spectrum canola oil), onions, celery and red pepper

Seafood salad or shrimp salad (mix Uncle Dan's package dressing with nonfat yogurt and use in place of mayonnaise). Add celery, red pepper and onions.

Vegetable salads using Uncle Dan's dressing as above, or olive oil and balsamic vinegar. You can add shrimp, or chunks of chicken or turkey. Just throw some chicken breasts in the oven for about 35 minutes at 350° and let them cook. Remove all the skin and fat, cut up the meat, and keep in a zip-lock bag for salads and sandwiches.

DINNERS

SOUPS

If you make a big pot of soup on the weekends, you will have something nutritious to eat all week. This is good for the modern family where mothers work and family members all get home at different hours. Each of the recipes makes a big pot. If you want to make less, just cut it in half. Most of the measurements are approximate.

MA ZIMBEROFF'S CHICKEN SOUP (DELICIOUS!) - quantity for one week

8 to 10 chicken breasts (skin and fat removed, bones okay)

1 large onion, chopped

2 cups chopped celery

2 cups sliced carrots

2 cups diced red potatoes

2 cups red or green bell peppers

Broccoli flowerets (or other vegetables such as zucchini)

6 blended tomatoes or 2 cans tomato sauce

1 cup whole wheat noodles or brown rice (optional)

3 to 4 Tablespoons Spike (available at health food stores)

2 to 3 Tablespoons Italian spices

Salt – small amount

Pepper to taste

Garlic to taste

Fill a 9-quart soup pot about two-thirds full of water and put chicken breasts in. Boil on high heat for about 5 minutes and skim off all the "junk" on top. Turn heat to low and simmer for about 25 minutes. Meanwhile begin chopping the vegetables while the chicken is cooking. After 25 minutes, remove all the chicken with a fork and let it cool. When the chicken has cooled enough to touch it, remove the bones. Cube the chicken and put it back into the soup. Add all the other ingredients and let it cook until the veggies are done - not soggy, but crunchy-soft. If you wish you can add some whole wheat spirals or brown rice. Then put the pot in the refrigerator, and heat up the day's serving amount. Do not keep reheating the whole pot because the veggies will overcook.

SEVEN-BEAN SOUP - quantity for one week
1 cup of each of the following:
yellow split peas
green split peas
lentils
red kidney beans
small soup beans (white)
lima beans
pinto beans

Wash beans well and drain in a large colander. Put in a large 9-quart soup pot and fill pot two-thirds full with water. Boil on high for 5 minutes and skim the "junk" off. Then cover and simmer for about 45 minutes, until the beans are tender, not mushy.
While it is cooking, begin cutting up vegetables:
2 cups onions
2 cups green peppers
3 cups celery
3 cups carrots
2 cups red peppers
2 cups chopped tomatoes.
When beans are tender, add vegetables and cook about 10 minutes, until they are just tender but not mushy. While they are cooking, add seasoning:
2 tsp. marjoram leaves
2 tsp. basil leaves

1 tsp. savory
1 tsp. thyme
Garlic to taste
4 Tablespoons Spike
Pepper to taste

Keep refrigerated and do not reheat whole pot; only individual servings.

DIANE'S DELICIOUS FRUIT SALAD
1 melon in balls
1 pineapple, chopped (using a pineapple corer makes it very easy)
6 apples, chopped
6 navel oranges, peeled and chopped
1 bunch of seedless grapes (cut in half if too big)
Fresh strawberries or frozen strawberries (no sugar added)
1 pkg. frozen blackberries (no sugar added)
1 pkg. mixed frozen berries
Any other fruit that you like

Mix all ingredients up in a large bowl and let them sit overnight. The next day toss with two forks and put into zip-lock bags. If everyone re-locks the bags, it will last almost two weeks (if not eaten up sooner). This is a real treat for kids and grown-ups alike. It is great for breakfast with cereal or omelets. This salad is a healthy snack or dessert also. The frozen berries are the secret ingredient that makes this fruit salad scrumptious!

APPENDIX 5

DAILY FOOD DIARY
(Use this diary just to stay conscious of your food choices.)

Date	Time	Food	Amount	Category

BIBLIOGRAPHY

Beyond Diet: The 28-Day Metabolic Breakthrough Plan. Martin Katahn. Berkley Publishing Group (1986).

Breaking Free from the Victim Trap: Reclaiming Your Personal Power. Diane Zimberoff. Wellness Press (1989; revised 2004).

Candida: The Epidemic of This Century Solved. Luc De Schepper. L D S Publications (1986).

Diets Don't Work. Bob Schwartz. Revised edition, Breakthru Publishing (1996).

Dr. Atkins' New Diet Revolution. Robert Atkins. Avon Books (2002).

Feeding the Hungry Heart: The Experience of Compulsive Eating. Geneen Roth. Plume; Reissue edition (1993).

Hypoglycemia: The Disease Your Doctor Won't Treat. Jeraldine Saunders & Harvey M. Ross. Kensington Publishing (1996 revised).

Mastering the Zone. Barry Sears. ReganBooks (1997).

No More Hot Flashes. Penny Wise Budoff. Warner Books (1984).

PMS: Premenstrual Syndrome and You: Next Month Can Be Different. Niels H. Lauersen & Eileen Stukane. Kensington Publishing (1984).

Potatoes Not Prozac. Kathleen DesMaisons. Simon & Schuster (1998).

Prescription for Nutritional Healing. Phyllis Balch & James Balch. Avery Publishing, 3rd Revised & Expanded edition (2000).

Recipes to Lower Your Fat Thermostat: The Official Companion to How to Lower Your Fat Thermostat and the New Neuropsychology of Weight Control. La Rene Gaunt. Vitality House International, 2nd edition (1992).

Self Esteem: A Family Affair. Jean Illsley Clarke. Hazelden (1998).

Sugar Blues. William Duffy. Warner Books, Reissue edition (1986).

The South Beach Diet. Arthur Agatston. Random House (2003).

Vitamin Bible. Earl Mindell. Warner Books, Revised edition (1991).

Women Who Love Too Much. Robin Norwood. Pocket, Reissue edition (1990).

Yeast Connection: A Medical Breakthrough. William G. Crook and Cynthia P. Crook. Knopf Publishing Group (1986).

PERSONAL TRANSFORMATION

Self-Improvement Audio Programs
by Diane Zimberoff

Audio Programs on CD

1. Codependency
2. Extinguishing Unwanted Behaviors
3. Healing and meditation
4. Prosperity
5. Self-esteem and Parenting
6. Self-hypnosis Program
7. Strengthening the Immune System
8. Visualization & Eliminating Stress

Order these and other audio programs today!

Call our office at 800-326-4418
or
Visit our online store
www.wellness-institute.org

Personal Transformation Meditations

The Chakras Meditation
2 CD set

FIRST CD
Track 1
INTRODUCTION TO MEDITATION
1. Creating Sacred Space
2. Benefits of Chakra Meditation
3. Quieting the Mind
4. Receiving a Spiritual Mantra

Track 2
ACTIVATING LOWER CHAKRAS
1. Connecting with the Earth
2. Power Animal's Message
3. Cleansing the Chakras
4. Release Energetic Drains
5. Connecting with Divine Presence

Track 3
ACTIVATING HIGHER CHAKRAS
1. Cleansing the Higher Chakras
2. Heart Space above the Head
3. Compassion for Humanity
4. Soul Retrieval
5. Aura Expansion & Healing Energy

SECOND CD
Track 1
SOUL RETRIEVAL MEDITATION
1. Discovering Soul-splits in each Chakra
2. Cleansing Soul Fragments
3. Reclaiming Soul Fragments
4. Hearing your Soul's Message
5. Embracing the Symbol in each Chakra
6. Sealing the Soul in each Chakra

Track 2
MIND - BODY - SPIRIT HEALING
1. Pranayama Breathing
2. Discovering the Glands, Hormones and Organs in each Chakra
3. Manifesting Healing in each Chakra
4. Affirmations for Mind-Body Healing
5. Focusing on specific areas for Increased Healing
6. Calling in your Healing Angels

Divine Mother and Power Animal Meditations

Track 1
CALLING IN THE DIVINE MOTHER

1. The Root Chakra - Lakshmi
2. The Sacral Chakra - Shakti
3. The Solar Plexus Chakra - Kali
4. The Heart Chakra - Durga
5. The Throat Chakra - Saraswati
6. The Third Eye Chakra - Parvati
7. The Crown Chakra – Narayani/Ishwari

Track 2
POWER ANIMAL MEDITATION

Discovering the Power Animal in each Chakra

Finding the individual message carried by each animal for your healing and personal growth

PERSONAL TRANSFORMATION

Breaking Free from the Victim Trap
Fourth printing 2004: over 30,000 books in print

This book has changed the lives of tens of thousands of readers.

It is written clearly and simply, yet carries a profound message of hope. The damage has been done, but the good news is that each of us can repair that damage.

The Victim Game is a family game taught to children in three ways.

The first is by direct example since one or more of the parents is usually a victim in families where this game is played.

Second, the child is programmed by the parent to be a victim.

Third, the victim behavior is reinforced by the parent until it becomes a permanent part of the child's identity.

The child goes through life then having one victim experience after another and each experience reinforces this person's victim position.

The Victim Game can be stopped and changed, but it takes (1) desire to change; (2) awareness; and (3) intensive therapy to change the subconscious programming.

Discount for quantity orders.
Call 800-326-4418, or visit the online store at:
www.wellness-institute.org

THE WELLNESS INSTITUTE

Now, BREAKING FREE from the VICTIM TRAP
The Audio Program

This CD is a companion experience to the book. It is not an audio reading of the book.

Discounts for quantity purchases.

Track 1
INTRODUCTION to BREAKING FREE from the VICTIM TRAP

1. The Law of Attraction
2. Healing through Relationships
3. Addiction to the Drama
4. Reclaiming Personal Power

Track 2
HEALING *VICTIM* CONSCIOUSNESS HYPNOTHERAPY EXPERIENCE

1. Discovering Your Safe Place
2. Identifying Current **Victim** Patterns
3. Discovering the Source of the **Victim**
4. Releasing the Feelings
5. Nurturing the Inner Child
6. Creating a New Healthy Pattern
7. Empowerment Affirmations

Track 3
HEALING VICTIM CONSCIOUSNESS
Beautiful Butterfly **(Bobbi Branch)**

Track 4
HEALING *RESCUER* CONSCIOUSNESS HYPNOTHERAPY EXPERIENCE

1. Discovering Your Safe Place
2. Identifying Current **Rescuer** Patterns
3. Discovering the Source of the **Rescuer**
4. Releasing the Feelings
5. Nurturing the Inner Child
6. Creating a New Healthy Pattern
7. Empowerment Affirmations

Track 5
HEALING RESCUER CONSCIOUSNESS
Sing Your Own Song **(Bobbi Branch)**

Track 6
HEALING *PERSECUTOR* CONSCIOUSNESS HYPNOTHERAPY EXPERIENCE

1. Discovering Your Safe Place
2. Identifying Current **Persecutor** Patterns
3. Discovering the Source of the **Persecutor**
4. Releasing the Feelings
5. Nurturing the Inner Child
6. Creating a New Healthy Pattern
7. Empowerment Affirmations

THE WELLNESS INSTITUTE
800-326-4418

$\mathcal{P}$ersonal $\mathcal{T}$ransformation $\mathcal{I}$ntensive
PTI

Find a PTI near you

www.PTIntensive.com

This is a profoundly healing group process, meeting for five weekend retreats over five months, in a loving environment. Do you long for these changes in your life?

Attract Healthy, Loving, Fulfilling Relationships
Belong to a new healthy, high-powered family • Develop close in-depth friendships instead of "cocktail party superficial phoniness" • Learn healthy support (not competition) • Learn to love yourself so you can love others

Experience Personal Growth and Transformation
Self-awareness • Higher consciousness • Self-discovery

Manifest Your Goals using the full power of your mind:
It's time to stop wanting things to happen in your life and time to start making things happen • Learn to use 100% of your mind to reach your full potential with a new goal-setting process • Discover your unconscious goals • Get clear on what you want • Become a member of a Master Mind Group

Improved Health with Powerful Stress Reduction Tools
Learn messages that your body is telling you • Release body hatred and shame • Relaxation Anchors • Heart-centered meditation • Conscious Breathing

Improved Finances
Prosperity and abundance principles • Master Mind groups • Learn the role of integrity in creating your abundance

Release Self -Defeating Patterns
Procrastination • "Victim, Rescuer, Persecutor" • Fear-based decisions (learn to make clear decisions) • Codependency • Unhealthy relationship patterns

Improved Communication Skills
Learn "The Clearing Process" • Stop "The Blame Game"

Take Full Responsibility for your Life!
Stop sabotaging yourself • Learn accountability and integrity • Release the shame which diminishes your self-esteem • Release self-judgment, self-blame

THE WELLNESS INSTITUTE
800-326-4418

CLEAN BREAK
Stop Smoking Program
With Hypnosis

CLEAN BREAK is a group stop-smoking program, consisting of four weekly classes. Use the power of hypnosis to help take control of unhealthy habits and replace them with new healthy ones.

The hypnosis included in this program helps you become a non-smoker by accessing the subconscious where habits are formed. Each of the four weekly sessions offers a hypnosis exercise that complements the material presented in that session. The exercises are repeated on an audiotape or CD provided for the participant to review daily throughout the seminar, increasing the exposure to suggestions for behavior modification and cognitive restructuring.

Developed by Diane Zimberoff
and offered exclusively
by The Wellness Institute

call 800-326-4418
to find a program provider in your area